MODERN WORLD NATIONS

Senegal

Janet H. Gritzner
South Dakota State University

Series Consulting Editor
Charles F. Gritzner
South Dakota State University

Philadelphia

Frontispiece: Flag of Senegal

Cover: Traditional hut used for grinding grain in a village in Senegal.

CHELSEA HOUSE PUBLISHERS

VP, NEW PRODUCT DEVELOPMENT Sally Cheney
DIRECTOR OF PRODUCTION Kim Shinners
CREATIVE MANAGER Takeshi Takahashi
MANUFACTURING MANAGER Diann Grasse

Staff for SENEGAL

EXECUTIVE EDITOR Lee Marcott
PRODUCTION EDITOR Noelle Nardone
SERIES DESIGNER Takeshi Takahashi
COVER DESIGNER Keith Trego
PHOTO RESEARCH 21st Century Publishing and Communications, Inc.
LAYOUT 21st Century Publishing and Communications, Inc.

A Haights Cross Communications ⌐ Company

http://www.chelseahouse.com

First Printing

1 3 5 7 9 8 6 4 2

Library of Congress Cataloging-in-Publication Data

Gritzner, Janet H.
    Senegal / Janet H. Gritzner.
        p. cm.—(Modern world nations)
Includes bibliographical references and index.
    ISBN 0-7910-8023-4
    1. Senegal—Juvenile literature. I. Title. II. Series.
DT549.22.G75 2004
966.3—dc22

                                                            2004014430

Table of Contents

Senegal

1

Introducing
Senegal

Senegal is a very special place. Few who have visited this West African country forget its unique sounds, smells, sights, and people. Although its people are of ancient lineage, today they show the mark of outside influences. Their religion is Islam, introduced from the Middle East, and their culture reveals the imprint of 50 years of French colonial influence.

Senegal is the westernmost nation of West Africa. It lies farther west than any European country except Iceland and lies only 1,800 miles (2,900 kilometers) from the Brazilian coast. It has a total area of 75,749 square miles (196,190 square kilometers), making it slightly smaller than the state of South Dakota. The country is bounded by the Atlantic Ocean to the west, Mauritania to the north, Mali to the east, and Guinea and Guinea-Bissau to the south. The Senegal River defines the northern border between

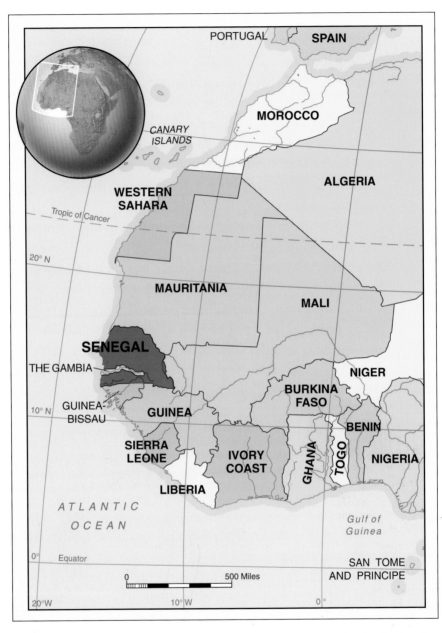

Senegal lies further west than any European country except Iceland. It is also the westernmost nation of West Africa and is bounded by the Atlantic Ocean to the west, Mauritania to the north, Mali to the east, and Guinea and Guinea-Bissau to the south.

Senegal and Mauritania. The Faleme River, a tributary of the Senegal River, delineates part of the eastern border with Mali.

The independent sliver-like nation of The Gambia forms a virtual enclave of 4,361 square miles (11,295 square kilometers) along the Gambia River in the southern part of Senegal. Except where it meets the Atlantic Ocean, the Gambia is entirely enveloped by Senegal's southwestern region. Its 200-mile (320-kilometer) east-to-west span physically and politically separates the drier northern part of Senegal from the wetter and more fertile region of the south.

Approximately one-fifth (19 percent) of the country is considered suitable for agricultural uses, one-third (32 percent) supports forest or savanna grassland cover, and the remaining half (48 percent) is largely desert and noncultivable.

Dakar is Senegal's capital, international gateway, and largest urban center, with a population of nearly 2.5 million. The sprawling city is located on Cap Vert (Cape Verde), a peninsula that juts into the Atlantic and is swept all year by trade winds from the sea. Its location on the continent's most westward reach places Dakar in a favorable position for trading with Europe and the Americas. This advantage has helped the city become the major trading center for all of West Africa.

Dakar is a city of great contrasts. It is home to shantytowns and modern high-rises; streets are crowded with cattle and Mercedes automobiles, and men and women whose lives have been shaped as much by tribal custom as by twenty-first century aspirations.

Senegal is a country of contrasting modern and traditional life styles. Modernity, often with a French flavor, is found in the cities and towns, especially those close to Dakar. Traditional modes are found more often among people in smaller and more remote towns and villages. In the country, many people are simply too poor to enjoy modern lifestyles and amenities.

Remote villages may seem to have little in common with urbanized Dakar, but most of Senegal truly is a mix of the modern and the old ways. Senegal is one of the world's poorer nations, yet although they are hard pressed economically, its people possess a rich and varied cultural life.

The country's Muslim character is imprinted on the landscape. One of the first things a visitor notices in Senegal is the towering minarets of the mosques. "Call to Prayer" wakens the country each day, as do roosters crowing and, even in a big city like Dakar, the sounds of sheep and goats. Thus, religion and ethnicity have shaped the character and personality of Senegalese people.

Senegal has a history of kingdoms, empires, brotherhoods, and colonial struggles (between and against colonizing powers). but compared with much of Africa, Senegal is a relatively modern state. The country has a tradition of moderation, progressiveness, stability, and democracy. Its economic life is tied to agriculture, fishing, and mining, but its fortunes are often subject to the whims of weather and the market. Life is hard for many, and, like many African countries, health concerns are a major issue. Although beset with many problems, Senegal has a bright future. Its economy is stable and on the upturn, showing steady growth in the past few years.

Through this book, you will travel to Africa, visiting a country where the humid tropics meet the desert. You will study the country through time and learn about its people, culture, government, and economy. You will see what it is like to live in Senegal today and what the future may bring.

2

Natural Environment

S enegal is a land of many contrasting environmental conditions. In this chapter, you will learn about its land and water features, weather and climate, flora and fauna, and environmental issues.

GEOLOGIC STRUCTURE AND LANDFORMS

Senegal's elevation extremes are the sea level shores of the Atlantic and the Fouta Djallon foothills, which top out at about 1,900 feet (580 meters). The topography is relatively flat except for low hills in the southeast. Senegal's 330-mile (530-kilometer) coastal plain is sandy from Saint-Louis to Dakar and swampy and muddy south of Dakar.

Geologically, Senegal is composed of two primary relief features. The first is a dissected, elevated region of folded and faulted rocks in the southeast. These are rocks of the ancient "African Shield." They are primarily quartzite, granite, and granite-like schists (rock

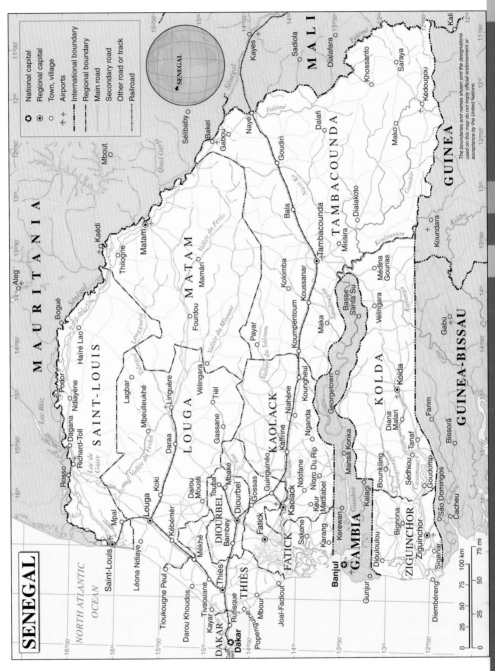

The topography of Senegal is relatively flat except for low hills in the southeast. Senegal's 330-mile (530-kilometer) coastal plain is sandy from Saint-Louis to Dakar and swampy and muddy south of Dakar.

that has a foliated structure of thin layers and can be split along approximately parallel planes). The second is a shallow sedimentary subsidence basin composed of clayey sandstones of varying thickness occupying the western and northeastern part of the country. This is the "Continental Terminal" formation, which occupies the largest part of the country. It consists of a low plateau and plains overlain by windblown sediments, alluvial (river-deposited) soil, and intermittent laterite (hard clayey soil high in iron content) hardcap. The country's principal mineral resources are phosphates and iron ore.

SOILS

Senegal's soils are dry and sandy in the north, iron-rich (ferrous) in the central regions, and highly leached (with nutrients removed) laterites in the South. In general, soil fertility is low and the soil is extremely vulnerable to wind and other forms of erosion.

Termite Mounds

One conspicuous feature of Senegal's soil landscape is the numerous termite mounds. Termites account for up to one-half of the biomass of the African plains. The continent is home to 400 species of termites, several of which are major crop pests in Senegal. Where the mounds are especially large or numerous, they can severely hinder farming operations.

Termite mounds are made of sun-baked mud. Inside the mound are a series of tunnels that exit through chimneys, which warm in the sun and draw cooler air and oxygen from the bottom of the mound. Mounds vary in size, depending on the termite species and on soil conditions. Some may be up to 30 feet (9 meters) tall, with nests extending down to 50 feet (15 meters) underground. In southeastern Senegal, mounds up to 20 feet (6 meters) tall dot the landscape. These nests can contain huge numbers of termites, with densities as high as 4 million termites per acre (9 million per hectare).

Termites use their saliva to cement soil particles that form the mounds, adding organic matter to the soil. In fact, there are termite savannas in which trees and shrubs grow in tufts in the enriched soil of termite nests. The value of termites is disputed. The insects consume vast quantities of organic matter, damage crops, and are blamed for increased soil erosion that may occur around termite mounds. On the other hand, termite colonies enhance soil fertility by transporting and concentrating fertile subsoil clays near the surface and by increasing soil aeration. African farmers often seek out termite mounds and plant crops around them, because crop yields usually are higher in these sites. Geologists have learned that mound samples are useful in prospecting for various metal ore deposits. Gold has been found in eastern Senegal by people testing termite mounds!

Termites also are an important food for many animals and birds and their mounds serve as lookouts for lions, cheetahs, and leopards. Abandoned mounds may serve as home to monitor lizards and other creatures.

WATER RESOURCES

Four major rivers flow westward through Senegal into the Atlantic. From north to south they are the Senegal, Saloum, Gambia (Gambie), and Casamance. These rivers are wide and meandering, with broad estuaries (water passages where the tide meets a river current) at their mouths. Lake Guiers (Lac de Guiers), the country's only natural lake, is located in the north. It is the principal source of drinking water for the Cap Vert region (Dakar and vicinity).

The Senegal is one of West Africa's most important rivers, with a length of 1,020 miles (1,641 kilometers) and a drainage basin encompassing 174,000 square miles (450,000 square kilometers). Two of the river's three headstreams rise in the Fouta Djallon highlands in Guinea, after which the river flows to the northwest and then to the west to drain into

The Faidherbe Bridge crosses the Senegal River at Saint-Louis. The bridge was named for the former governor of French Senegal, Commander Louis Faidherbe.

the Atlantic. For 515 miles (829 kilometers) of its course, it forms the boundary between Mauritania and Senegal. Two dams have been built on the river: an antisalinity dam at Diama completed in 1987 and a flow-controlled hydroelectric dam at Manantali completed in 1988. The river has an average annual flow of 23 billion cubic meters. Unfortunately, only 4 or 5 billion cubic meters of flow are being used, leaving a large amount of the country's water supply lost as it flows into the sea.

The Saloum complex of valleys and ponds provides water seasonally, although it has a problem of seawater incursion far upstream at low-flow stage. Except for its easternmost origins,

The Saloum River is one of the four major rivers that flow westward through Senegal into the Atlantic Ocean. All of these rivers are wide and meandering as is shown by this view of the Saloum River.

the Gambia River is surrounded by the country of the Gambia. The annual mean flow of the Gambia River is 10 billion cubic meters. Only a small portion of the river is located in Senegal. In the south, the Casamance River offers relatively low flows. During most of the year, there are seawater incursions in its middle and lower channels.

Most of Senegal's water lies underground, trapped in an aquifer (layer) of sediments. On a national scale, groundwater resources are very abundant, except in the Tambacounda region. The potential for exploiting this resource is highly variable by region, however, depending on the capacity, depth, and degree of mineralization of the aquifers.

ECOLOGICAL REGIONS

Senegal can be divided into nine geographic or ecological regions. They are the Senegal River Valley, the Long Coast, West Central Agricultural Domain, Pastoral Domain, Casamance, Eastern Plains, Eastern Transition Zone, Dakar Region, and Shield Ecoregion.

The Senegal River

The Senegal River flows through Sahelian (desert fringe) landscapes of Senegal, Mali, and Mauritania. Here, it creates a unique and complex environment largely directed by what happens on the floodplain. At one time, an extensive forest dominated the river valley. Today, forest remnants are restricted to shallow depressions and levees along the river. Many are designated forest reserves.

Over the centuries, local peoples cleared most of floodplain, known as the Walo, for traditional subsistence agriculture and, more recently, for large irrigation projects. Some farmers practice flood recessional agriculture on the heavy alluvial soils (those with organic material deposited by water) found on the banks of the river's many channels. The Senegal River has been the target for large development projects that have had mixed results. Two planned dams were completed by 1987, but the benefits from irrigation projects and hydroelectric power have been slow in coming and negative ecological consequences are now being felt. They include an increase in parasitic diseases, a decline in food production (some of which is caused by disruption of traditional flood recessional agriculture), a decrease of dry-season pasture, and stress imposed on remaining river woodlands.

The Long Coast

The Long Coast (Niayes Region) is a narrow coastal belt containing small swamps, oases, creeks, channels, and mudflats. This unique ecoregion is located along the country's northern coast. It offers a variety of microenvironments formed by the region's humid maritime (sea) air and adequate moisture and a land surface characterized by both active and stabilized coastal and inland sand dunes. Between the dunes are depressions called *niayes*, which harbor complex and rich flora, or plant life. This region is famous for its market gardening: More than two-thirds of the country's vegetable production comes from the niayes. The surrounding red-colored continental sand dunes support a shrub savanna, used for centuries as grazing lands by pastoralists (people who raise livestock).

West Central Agricultural Domain

This region includes the Groundnut (Peanut) Basin and more recently colonized agricultural lands to the south and east. The Groundnut Basin is Senegal's commercial agricultural center. It is an area of interior dunes with level or slightly undulating topography. Two centuries of peanut cultivation and a large rural population have contributed to the general degradation of this basin's sandy soils. Woodlands that once covered the area have been replaced completely with a tree parkland dominated by acacias. The central Sine and Saloum area to the south forms a transition from intensive peanut production to multicrop production of the southern Saloum. It encompasses the traditional Serer agricultural lands and the more recently colonized Wolof and Serer lands to the east.

Peanut cultivation has been expanding rapidly to the south-east since the 1950s. The region has higher rainfall and a longer growing season than most of the Groundnut Basin, but it lacks the heavy mantle of sand characteristic of the Groundnut Basin's best peanut-growing areas. The so-called new lands (*terres nueves*) are possibly the fastest-changing environment in Senegal. Natural land cover is being converted rapidly to rain-fed agriculture. If the trend continues, agricultural crops will replace the remaining natural vegetation in a few decades. Woodlands are the primary source of fuel for home cooking and heating, and they are also important areas for livestock grazing and foraging.

Pastoral Domain—The Ferlo and Southern Sandy Pastoral Ecoregion

Ferlo is an inland continuation of the western plains and is semidesert. It can be divided into two distinct subregions: sandy Ferlo to the west and the ferruginous (iron-bearing) Ferlo to the east. Sandy Ferlo is the heart of Senegal's woodland pastoral zone. It comprises a vast area of ancient dunes now reduced to terrain of flat or gently rolling windblown sands.

The ferruginous zone, or ferruginous Ferlo, is distinguished from the sandy Ferlo by its gravelly soils, which overlie exposed laterites. The local relief (terrain) is more pronounced, dissected by valleys that contribute to considerable variation in natural vegetation. It is an area of generally poorer pastureland. As in the sandy Ferlo, the presence or absence of water constitutes a primary factor that determines the intensity of human and animal pressure on the natural resources.

At one time, Ferlo was covered by a savanna landscape marked by grasslands and a diverse tree species. Today, the vegetation is much more open and lacks diversity. Many observers have reported on the degradation of vegetation in the Ferlo over the past 50 years. They point to a combination of factors including low rainfall, pressure of a growing livestock population (especially the concentration around wells called boreholes), and the breakdown of the traditional pastoral system among the Peul (local livestock raisers).

The sandy pastoral zone in the south is similar to the sandy Ferlo of the north, except that it has significantly higher rainfall. The area still is lightly populated, but it is feeling the effects of aggressive agricultural expansion. This zone is part of Senegal's extensive pastoral region and has more reliable and productive grasslands than do regions to the north and east. It contains large pastoral and forest reserves set aside by the colonial government in the 1930s. Northern pastoralists use these grazing lands regularly for dry-season grazing. Today, the predominant vegetation cover is shrub and tree savanna.

The Casamance

The Casamance is known for its lush forest landscapes, valley bordered by palms, and wet rice fields. Casamance is the region located south of the Gambia River and is distinguished from other regions by high seasonal rainfall, a well-developed drainage system, iron-rich (ferralitic) soils, and relatively dense and diverse vegetation. It is home to a number of ethnic groups and is separated physically from the rest of Senegal by the Gambia. Today, Casamance is showing signs of the same type of degradation taking place elsewhere in the country. Pressures are coming mainly from expanding agriculture and charcoal production.

Eastern Transition Ecoregion

This region is similar to the area of agricultural expansion, except that it is farther from the heavily populated Groundnut Basin and lateritic plateaus are common. The region is an important source for fuel wood, mainly in the form of charcoal. Typically, charcoal producers come through an area and reduce woody cover by half. The region's eastern margin remains largely unaffected, but, with the growing appetite for fuel wood, it is an area at risk.

Dakar Region

The Dakar Region is the country's smallest ecoregion. Here, more than anywhere else in the country, the human imprint dominates the landscape. Cap Vert was formed in part by ancient volcanic activity, and exposure to southwesterly winds is responsible for the peninsula's greenness—a sharp contrast to the yellow dunes to the north. The land cover type is a mix of woody species, shrubs, and herbaceous (leafy) species. Gnarled baobab trees in small or large groupings are found within the Dakar Region.

Shield Ecoregion

This lightly populated region in the southeast part of the country is far from Senegal's population centers and has limited agricultural potential. A large part of this area falls within the Niokolo-Koba National Park, which contains some of the most unspoiled arid and semiarid types of flora and fauna left in Africa.

Geology is what sets this region apart. Exposed ancient rock formations yield Senegal's only mineral resources. Numerous metallic and nonmetallic minerals, including gold, iron, marble, diamonds, copper, uranium, and manganese, have been found. Several new mining towns have appeared, and newly paved roads are opening the region for development.

WEATHER AND CLIMATE

Across Senegal, rainfall is widely dispersed in both location and timing. The country lies on the equatorial side of 17 degrees north latitude, placing it well within the tropics. Temperatures are high throughout the year, and the country experiences pronounced wet and dry seasons. The coastal area is remarkably cool considering the latitude.

Dakar ranks as one the coolest, breeziest spots in West Africa. Average temperature ranges in Dakar are from 64 to 79°F (18 to 26°C) in January to 75 to 90°F (24 to 32°C) in September. Interior temperatures are higher than along the coast, but the humidity is lower.

Rainfall patterns in West Africa are more unpredictable than in other parts of the continent. Senegal's rainfall can be variable, and the country has experienced long dry periods. During the 1970s and 1980s, rainfall declined significantly; it has, however, increased in recent years. The quantity for a certain year may be normal, but the rainy season may vary greatly in beginning, length, and end, especially in central and northern Senegal.

Annual rainfall is almost entirely limited to the summer wet season, which lasts up to six months (May to November) in the south and decreases to three months (July to September) in the north. Amounts of rainfall also increase from south to north. Average rainfall varies from more than 60 inches (1,500 millimeters) in the southwest to just under 12 inches (300 millimeters) in the northwest. Dakar gets more than 24 inches (600 millimeters) annually, most of which falls in June and October.

Senegal lies in the zone of the northeast tradewinds, and a wind called the harmattan affects the country most. This wind can blast West Africa's Sahel region for days at a time. During the dry season, it blows as a hot dust-laden blast of air from the Sahara Desert. Gale force squalls and even occasional tornadoes can occur at the beginning and end of the rainy season. If a harmattan is unusually persistent, its parched winds will dry out both crops and water sources.

VEGETATION

Senegal is the most biologically diverse country in the Sahel—the southern edge of the Sahara Desert that stretches across most of Africa. Although Senegal is a small country, it is part of three bioclimatic zones: the Sahelian, the Sudanian, and the Guinean zones. Vegetation change, caused by the extreme annual rainfall differences between the semiarid north and the wetter south, is pronounced. Although mostly covered with savanna, the country becomes semidesert in the Sahel region of the north and northeast and forested in the southwest.

The driest zone is the Sahelian Region in northern Senegal. Here, an average of 12 to 20 inches (300 to 500 millimeters) of precipitation fall annually. Early seasonal rains, which usually begin in July, transform the landscapes for a short period of time into lush green grazing land, which is its primary use.

The driest zone of the arid Sahel region lies in northern Senegal. Long distances are often traveled to reach the wells, which are few in number. Animals must be given enough water to last to the next water source.

By late September, however, rain ceases and grasses quickly dry out. Shrub savannas, shrub and tree savannas, and bushlands dominate this land. The woody cover, mostly umbrella-shaped acacia trees, rarely exceeds 25 feet (8 meters) in height.

The Sudanian Region lies to the south of the Sahelian zone and covers about two-thirds of central and southern Senegal. Typical vegetation types include the savanna woodland and the dry woodland. Most areas in this region receive 30 to 60 inches (750 to 1,500 millimeters) of precipitation annually. Here, rain is spread over five to six months, mostly in July through

September. With the onset of the rainy season, the landscape is transformed rapidly by vigorous vegetation growth. During the low-sun "winter" season, conditions dry out. For a period of six to seven months, the sky can remain cloudless for weeks on end and the land becomes parched.

About 80 species of trees have been identified in this region. They include acacia and species of the baobab. Human occupation has greatly modified the vegetation of the region, particularly in the Groundnut Basin.

The Guinean Region proper can only be found in the extreme southwest corner of Senegal. It is a region of the semi-evergreen dense forest. It has been reduced to a few communities. Forests have been cleared and replaced with the cultivation of rice, manioc, and peanuts. The Guinean Region encompasses the areas of average annual rainfall exceeding 60 inches (1,500 millimeters). Despite the high rainfall, this region has a distinct seven- to eight-month dry season that distinguishes it from Africa's equatorial region that is moist year-round.

Unique Aspects of Senegal's Vegetation
Baobab Trees

Tourist ads often call Senegal the "Land of baobab trees." The African baobab grows naturally in most countries south of the Sahara, but the baobab forests of Senegal are a prominent landscape feature. The baobab truly is a national tree revered in Senegal. It is not cut for firewood or other use.

Called the most valuable tree in Africa, the baobab has multiple uses. Its fruit, which grows up to a foot (30 centimeters) long, can be sucked or soaked in water to make a refreshing drink. Bark is pounded to make rope, mats, baskets, paper, and cloth. Leaves can be boiled and eaten in stews, and glue can be made from the pollen. According to some experts, every part of the tree has medicinal use. Baobab trees are featured in fertility rites and in rituals in respect of ancestors and are even used as burial places for *griots* (performers).

The African baobab tree grows naturally in most countries south of the Sahara, but in Senegal, they are a prominent feature of the landscape. They are not cut for firewood or cut down for any other purpose.

The baobab is an odd-looking tree, although beautiful in an angular way. When it loses its leaves, as happens during the dry season, its spreading branches look like roots sticking up into the air. As the story of the baobab goes, an angry god yanked up a normal tree, turned it upside down, and shoved it back into the ground. It is called "bottle tree," because its thick trunk is made of tissues saturated with water. Well suited to drought-prone climates, the baobab can hold more than 31,701 gallons (120,000 liters) of water in its trunk.

Baobabs have large whitish flowers that open at night. Fruits are pendulous (hanging), with a velvetlike coating. Baobabs can live 1,000 to 2,000 years, becoming enormous, and are very difficult to kill. When burned or stripped of their bark, they form new bark and continue growing. When they do die, they rot from the inside and suddenly collapse, leaving a heap of fibers, which makes many people think that they don't die but simply disappear.

Acacias

Within a housing compound, one is likely to find varieties of acacia trees that provide year-round shade for outdoor living. These trees are not cut, and their rounded green profiles usually are the first sign of a settlement ahead. One variety of acacia enriches the soil with nitrogen and other nutrients; it has a positive effect on the growth of peanut plants, so local farmers protect the trees.

In Senegal, the indigenous agricultural, woodland, and pastoral system takes advantage of the benefits provided by acacia species. One variety sheds its leaves at the beginning of the wet season. This permits enough light to allow sorghum and millet (two grasses that produce grains) to grow, yet it also provides enough shade to reduce the effects of intense heat. In the dry season, the tree's long taproots draw nutrients from beyond the reach of other plants. The tree also fixes, or extracts, nitrogen from the air, thus enriching the soil and improving crop yields. In the wet season, the fallen leaves provide mulch that enriches the topsoil, as well as providing highly nutritious forage (food for animals). The dung of livestock that feed on leaves and the residue of the cereal crops also enriches the soil. These benefits are extremely important in places where few alternatives exist for improving soil fertility, crop yields, and animal nutrition.

Bushfires

In Senegal, bushfires are a controversial subject. They are often cited as a major cause of degradation of forest resources. Bushfires play a very important and beneficial role in savanna ecosystems, however. The number and density of fires are highest in the savanna woodlands of eastern and southeastern Senegal. Here, herders start fires to promote new growth of nutritious grasses. Agricultural fires are common in the late dry season in the Casamance, and they are set all year in the Senegal River Valley to remove agricultural residue from irrigated rice fields. Bushfires are least frequent in the grasslands of the Ferlo and in the Groundnut Basin.

ANIMAL LIFE

Senegal's native animal life is typical of Africa's Sahel Region. Habitat has been destroyed for much of the original wildlife, and poaching, deforestation, and desertification (creation of desert conditions through human action) threaten remaining wildlife populations. Animals such as the ostrich, chimpanzee, wild dog, cheetah, African manatee, African elephant, giant eland, and red-fronted gazelle are close to extinction.

Senegal's parks and reserves play a critical role in the preservation of these species and other wildlife. The country has made a great effort to create a national park and nature reserve system that serves as the basis for a growing ecotourism (environmental tourism). At present, there are six national parks and eight reserves, totaling 8,525 square miles (22,080 square kilometers).

Popular National Parks

Parc National du Niokolo-Koba, Senegal's major park, is located in the southeastern corner of the country. The park covers 3,525 square miles (9,130 square kilometers) and offers a rich and varied landscape, with a concentration of almost all vegetation and animals of the West African savanna. Registered as a world heritage and an international biosphere site, the park has varied plant life and contains nearly 350 species of birds and 80 species of mammals, including lions, leopards, and elephants. It is also home to bushbucks, waterbucks, green monkeys,

Senegal's national parks play a critical role in the preservation of many species. A popular national park is the Parc National du Niokolo-Koba in the southeastern part of the country. These black-faced vervet monkeys are among the 80 species of mammals that can be found there.

patas (or hussar) monkeys, warthogs, baboons, roan antelopes, buffaloes, hartebeest, hippopotamuses, and crocodiles.

Parc National des Oiseaux du Djoudj (Birds of Djoudj National Park) is one the world's major bird reserves. It is located 37 miles (about 60 kilometers) north of Saint-Louis on the Senegal River. The park extends over 29,653 acres (12,000 hectares), which includes part of the river, many channels, lakes, basins, and marshes, as well as surrounding zones of savanna. It has a permanent water level, which attracts many species of bird. Migrating birds, particularly waterfowl, return from Europe in large numbers each winter. Each year, an estimated 3 million birds visit the park, where more than 400 species have been counted.

Antelopes are among the wildlife that can be seen in Senegal's national park and nature reserve system.

Parc National de la Basse Casamance is located in the lower Casamance. It offers a wide variety of habitats: forest, open savanna, mud banks, and mangrove swamp. Some animals living in the park are buffalo, bushbuck, duiker, hyena, mongoose, monkey, porcupine, and a wide variety of birds.

Parc Nationale de la Langue de Barbarie is located on the southern point of the Langue de Barbarie, about 12 miles (20 kilometers) south of Saint-Louis. The 4,942-acre (2,000-hectare) park is a refuge for many water birds, primarily cormorants, pink flamingos, pelicans, herons, and ducks.

Parc National de Sine Saloum is a wild region of mangrove swamps, lagoons, forests, dunes, and sand islands. Large mammals are rare, but there are monkeys and a wide variety of birds.

ENVIRONMENTAL ISSUES

The most significant of Senegal's many environmental issues are deforestation, overgrazing, soil erosion, desertification, overfishing, and poaching of wildlife. Charcoal production sites exist in woodlands throughout Senegal, and they represent the most significant factor leading to the rapid decline of forest resources. Natural forests have shrunk 7 to 8 percent or more during the past 15 years. Drought and increased salinity have resulted in high mangrove mortality, and drought, overgrazing, and subsequent loss of plant cover expose soils to water erosion during violent downpours.

The growing population has put pressure on the country's shrinking forest and vegetation cover, and inappropriate use of fertilizers has contributed to the degradation of already fragile soils, with a resulting decline in crop harvests. Degradation of water resources, especially from saline intrusion and pollution of subterranean waters with pesticides and other pollutants, has increased steadily.

Desertification

Desertification generally is viewed as an advanced stage of land degradation. The United Nations has defined it as "diminution or destruction of the biological potential of the land that can lead ultimately to desert-like conditions." Desertification in the northern part of the country is an ever-increasing problem only partially alleviated by the Manantali Dam on the Senegal River. It is the result of human and environmental causes. Changes in settlement patterns, increased population growth, drought, erosion, deforestation, overcultivation, and overgrazing of land are just some of the contributing factors.

Natural Hazards

Senegal is subject to seasonal floods, periodic droughts that are often lengthy and severe, and sandstorms. Overall, however, the country is relatively free of natural calamities. It experiences few violent storms and is free of earthquakes and volcanic activity.

3

History

S enegal's history is filled with kingdoms, empires, brotherhoods, and colonial struggles. This history begins with the first popu- lations that settled in Senegal. Beginning in the mid-eighth century, the Sahel prospered from trans-Saharan trade. From this activity grew several culturally and politically dynamic cities and kingdoms. In the European Middle Ages, parts of Senegal belonged to the empires of Ghana, Mali, and Songhai and to the kingdoms of Tekrur and Jolof.

GREAT EMPIRES OF WEST AFRICA
Empire of Ghana

The first great Sahelian kingdom was Ghana. Ancient Ghana encompassed what is now northern Senegal, a large part of Mauritania, and western Mali. Although it originated in the late fourth century, Ghana became a major regional power only near the end of the millennium (500–1000 A.D.). The state originally was formed by Berbers (Caucasian peoples of North Africa) and built on the southern edge of a Berber settlement.

In time, Ghana came to be dominated by the Soninke, a Mande-speaking people living in the region bordering the southern Sahara. They built their capital city, Kumbi Saleh, on the edge of the Sahara, and it soon became an important stop on trans-Saharan trade routes. Arabic travelers wrote of the magnificence of Ghana, its court, its kings covered with gold and jewels, and its army rich with thousands of archers. Caravans from Ghana regularly crossed the Sahara loaded with salt, copper, ivory, and brilliant cloth.

By the eleventh century, Ghana began to lose its dominance over the region. Mining of new gold fields at Bure (modern Guinea) began, out of the commercial reach of Ghana, and new trade routes were opening up farther east. Also, Ghana became the target of attacks by the Sosso ruler Sumanguru, and out of this conflict, in 1235, the Malinke people emerged under the leadership of a new ruler, Sundiata Keita. Soon, Ghana was totally eclipsed by the Mali Empire.

There were a number of reasons for Ghana's decline, including loss of trading monopoly, effects of drought, and pressures from outside forces. According to an Arab tradition, Berber Muslims from the north invaded Ghana. Another interpretation is that this Berber influence was gradual and did not involve a military takeover. The once-great empire split into a number of small, often feuding kingdoms. Out of this disorder came the great Mali Empire.

Empire of Mali

During the thirteenth century, the Empire of Mali arose to the east under Emperor Sundiata Keita and expanded to include Tekrur and most of the rest of Senegal. Mali was not a true empire; rather, it was the center of a sphere of influence. It spanned modern-day Guinea, Burkina Faso, Senegal, Mali, Mauritania, Niger, and Nigeria. As with Ghana, Mali emerged from trade dominance on routes from sub-Saharan Africa to eastern and northern Africa.

Mali monopolized the especially lucrative gold trade, which largely moved up the Niger River. The Mali Empire lasted from about 1235 to 1400 A.D.

According to African oral histories, Mali had been a state inside the Ghanaian empire. After Ghana fell, Mali rose to greatness under the leadership of a legendary king named Sundiata, the "Lion King." Sundiata seized the major territories through which gold was traded and thus laid the empire's foundation. He also introduced the cultivation and weaving of cotton. Later, another great leader named Mansa Musa extended the empire. After his death, however, his sons could not hold the empire together. The smaller states it had conquered broke off, and the empire crumbled.

Empire of Songhai

As Mali's power waned, Songhai asserted its independence. The dates for the empire of Songhai are between 1350 and 1600 A.D. and in the late fifteenth century, the whole territory became a part of that empire. Located in northern Nigeria, Songhai had been an important trade center within Mali's empire. Great Songhai kings such as Sunni Ali Ber and Askia Mohammed Toure extended the Songhai kingdom farther than Ghana or Mali and brought an organized system of government. Stretching from the Senegal and Gambia rivers in the far west and incorporating part of Hausaland (Nigeria) in the east, Songhai was the largest and most powerful kingdom in medieval West Africa. The riches of the gold and salt mines drew invaders, however, and, in 1591, a Moroccan army attacked the capital. The Songhai Empire, already weakened by internal political struggles, went into decline.

EMPIRES AND KINGDOMS OF SENEGAL

Empires and kingdoms also evolved within the borders of Senegal. The Kingdom of Tekrur and the Empire and Kingdom of Jolof had extensive power and influence in the region.

Kingdom of Tekrur

The Toucouleur settled in the central Senegal River valley in the ninth century. From 900 A.D. to 1250 A.D., the large Toucouleur kingdom of Tekrur, centered at Podor, dominated the valley. In time, the Kingdom of Tekrur was claimed by both the Ghana and Mali empires. The Tekrur kingdom is known for its early acceptance of Islam. In 1049, War Jabi, King of Tekrur, became a Muslim. The majority of Toucouleur subjects followed him, making them the first group in the region to convert to Islam. For a time, Tekrur was the southern end of a large Berber Muslim state that spanned the Sahara and was centered in Morocco.

Empire and Kingdom of Jolof

Wolof history in Senegal dates to about the twelfth century. According to oral traditions, the Wolof people migrated west from Mali to the coast after the defeat of the Empire of the Ghana. The Jolof kingdom of Senegal was founded between 1150 and 1350 A.D.

While the Mali Empire was at its height, the Jolof kingdom flourished in the region between the Senegal River and modern day Dakar, growing into an empire. It was made up of a number of states (Wolof kingdoms). These kingdoms later split from Jolof, which remained a kingdom until conquered by the French. The kingdoms of Saloum, Sine, and Biffeche continue today, along with tributary monarchies like Gandiaye, and the hereditary princes of Bethio and Jolof (whose kingdoms no longer exist) are still locally revered. The region was conquered by the French during the nineteenth century and, in 1886, the last Wolof king was killed in an insurrection.

EARLY EUROPEAN TRADERS

In the mid-1440s, Portuguese explorers reached the mouth of the Senegal River; it and the Gambia River were used as routes to the interior. Trading stations were established at the mouths of the Senegal and Casamance rivers and on Gorée Island and at Rufisque, both located near present-day Dakar.

In the seventeenth century, the Dutch and the French traders replaced the Portuguese, and throughout the seventeenth and eighteenth centuries the coast of Senegal was a major landing point for the transatlantic and European trades in ivory, gold, and slaves. Of all European trading activities, the African slave trade was the most active and abominable.

SLAVERY AND THE SLAVE TRADE

Slavery has a long history in Senegal. Economic power of the old native kingdoms of Senegal was rooted in the labor of slaves and serfs. It is said that for one free man there was one slave; in certain areas, the ratio was much higher, with as many as 16 slaves for each free adult. The Toucouleur had slaves as far back as the eleventh century. The Serers, one of the ancient peoples of Senegal, adopted slavery in the thirteenth century. Most slaves were servants or worked as agricultural laborers.

The African slave trade as big business began in the 1520s, when Portuguese merchants began to supply Caribbean plantations with African labor. It became the major source of military power and wealth for kingdoms and states of precolonial Senegal. As colonial empires developed rapidly across the Atlantic, African slaves were exported to America and the Caribbean in large numbers. In 1600, 300,000 slaves were shipped to America. In the course of the seventeenth century, Africa exported an estimated 1.5 million slaves. This figure reached 6.5 million during the eighteenth century.

Slave Markets

The largest trade centers in West Africa were in The Gambia and Guinea, but Senegal also had important markets. Senegal benefited from its coastal access and its border on Moorish (Arab or Berber) regions. Saint-Louis, located at the mouth of the Senegal River and with easy access to the interior, was one of the busiest trade centers. Bakel, a city in the upper Senegal River Valley, was huge slave market mainly supplied with Bambara captives.

The lack of a sandbar along the small coastline of the Cap Vert helped the development of the slave-trading posts of Rufisque, Portudal, and Joal. On Karabane Island, at the mouth of the Casamance River, the Captives' House (as distinct from a slave house) is still the most important building on the island, although it now is in ruin. The most famous slave trade site, however, is Gorée Island off the coast from Dakar. Despite its current popularity as a tourist attraction, Gorée was a very minor outpost.

Gorée Island

Gorée Island is Senegal's most famous tourist attraction. The historical site has come to symbolize the African slave trade, even though there is debate over how many slaves actually departed from the island. Gorée was one of the places where captives were gathered, locked up, and then taken aboard ships for transit to destinations overseas.

Tiny Gorée Island lies about two miles (three kilometers) off the coast of Dakar, and its proximity to the city makes it a good day trip for tourists. From 1444 to 1817, Gorée changed ownership four times: It was claimed by the Portuguese, Dutch, French, and British and eventually was returned to the French. The island offered good moorage and security and was ideally located for trade with Europe and the Americas. It was so well thought of that in 1785 the governor of Senegal moved his residence there.

Much of the island's charm is the surviving bits and pieces of its colonial history, and, with tourism in mind, it is now home to three museums, including the IFAN Historical Museum and the recently refurbished Maison des Esclaves (Slave House). Gorée has about 1,000 residents, no paved roads, and no cars. The Slave House was built in 1775 as a

Gorée Island, near Dakar, Senegal, was a minor outpost in the West African slave trade. The Slave House was built in 1775 and is said to be one of several sites on the island where Africans were brought to be loaded into ships bound for the New World.

trader's house and, according to local lore, a holding facility for slaves. Tourists can walk through dimly lit "dungeons" and be reminded of Senegal's involvement in the slave trade.

The End of Slavery

In 1827, the slave trade was banned north of the Equator by international agreement. The slave trade was slow to die, however. One interesting story is how, in 1846, Gorée Island lent shelter to 250 slaves taken from a slave ship off the coast of Angola. After three years on Gorée, they settled in Gabon, where they founded Libreville, capital of modern Gabon.

Finally, by the Decree of April 27, 1848, slavery was abolished in the French colonies. This freed not only slaves working French plantations but also slaves owned by Wolof, Serers, and other groups. Because the French had little control over groups in the interior at this time, the edict had little effect. In 1849, the French governor established "villages of liberty" at several locations near Saint-Louis. In the 1880s, several others were founded along the Senegal River Valley and the upper reaches of the Gambia.

THE FRENCH

France has had a lengthy and often turbulent relationship with Senegal. The French established a post at the mouth of the Senegal River in 1638. Two decades later, they founded Saint-Louis on an island near the original settlement. This marked the beginning of an era of colonization that ended with Senegal's independence in 1960. The town of Saint-Louis was named as a tribute to Louis XIII, king of France. It became the first permanent French settlement in Senegal, offering a good harbor and strategic defense.

In 1677, the French captured Gorée Island from the Dutch and, for a time, it became the main French naval base in West Africa. From 1667 to 1720, the Royal Company of Senegal extended French influence far into the interior, increasing the export of slaves, ivory, and gum arabic (used as glue or food thickener).

During the Seven Years' War (1756–1763), Great Britain captured all French posts in Senegal, returning only Gorée in 1763. Conquered territories were joined with British holdings along the Gambia River to form the short-lived colony of Senegambia, Britain's first African colony. During the American

Revolutionary War (1775–1783), France regained its posts but surrendered Gorée to Britain in 1783 under the Treaty of Paris. During the Napoleonic Wars, Britain again captured France's holdings in Senegal but returned them in 1815. At this time, the French presence was limited to Saint-Louis, Gorée, and Rufisque. During the first half of the nineteenth century, there was little contact with the interior, where trade was oriented inland toward the Sahara.

As part of a French policy of assimilation, inhabitants of Saint-Louis and Gorée elected a deputy to the national assembly in Paris from 1848 to 1852 and (joined by the inhabitants of Rufisque and Dakar) from 1871 to independence in 1960. The French built a fort in Dakar in 1857 to better serve merchants in the area. It was not until 1865 that they subdued much of Senegal. Even then, it was only with a policy of respecting local customs.

CONQUERING THE INTERIOR

Although European contact with the Wolof began in about the middle of the fifteenth century, it did not have major significance until nearly 300 years later. In the 1850s, the French launched their first serious attempts to conquer the Wolof kingdoms, primarily to protect their economic interests. During his short 10-year period as governor from 1854 to 1865 (except for 1862), Captain Louis Faidherbe conquered Walo and Cayor and extended French influence along the Casamance River. He also established schools for Africans and halted the westward expansion of El Haj Umar Tall, the Toucouleur leader of the Tijanes Muslim brotherhood. Umar Tall was waging a large-scale holy war that started in the early 1850s, and he died fighting the French. At about the same time, Toucouleur *marabout* (religious leader) Ma Ba Jaaxu conquered the pagan Mandinke on the Gambia River and Wolof and Serer groups to the north. He converted two powerful Wolof kings to

Islam, thus beginning the mass conversion of the Wolof to Muslim beliefs.

COLONIAL PERIOD

By the end of the century, the Wolof were completely subjugated and the French colonial administration was fully implemented. During this same period, and in part in reaction to French pressures and conquests, the Wolof rapidly adopted Islam. In 1895, Senegal was made a French colony, with its capital at Saint-Louis. France did not actually control all of the Senegal of today until 1904. By the early twentieth century, the French had expanded their control into neighboring territories. In 1908, Dakar became the capital of the territories of French West Africa, but the capital of Senegal stayed in Saint-Louis.

Dakar grew as an administrative center, helped by port improvements that attracted business from Rufisque. Under French colonial rule, Senegal's trade was reoriented toward the coast. The country's output of peanuts increased dramatically and railroads were built, most notably the line from Dakar to Bamako (in present-day Mali). During World War II, Senegal was aligned with the Vichy regime from 1940 to 1942 but then joined the Free French. In 1946, Senegal and the rest of French West Africa became part of the French Union and French citizenship was extended to all Senegalese. After World War II, Senegal became a French Overseas Territory.

INDEPENDENCE

In late 1958, after Charles de Gaulle came to power in France, Senegal became an autonomous republic within the French Community. The breakup of French West Africa was underway. Senegal joined French Sudan to form the Mali Federation. The federation gained independence in 1960 but broke up two months later, and Senegal and French Sudan (renamed the Republic of Mali) proclaimed independence.

Léopold Sédar Senghor, an internationally known poet, politician, and statesman, was elected Senegal's first president in August 1960.

SENGHOR'S PRESIDENCY

At the time of independence, power was fairly evenly divided between the country's president, Léopold Senghor, and its prime minister, Mamadou Dia. In December 1962, Dia staged an unsuccessful coup; he was arrested and early in 1963, a new constitution was written giving the president much additional power.

Léopold Sédar Senghor is the "Founding Father of Senegal." He is said to be thoroughly French and thoroughly Senegalese. Senghor was a Catholic leading a predominately Muslim population but was able to lead a truly peaceful transition from colonialism to independence. Highly respected in France, Senghor was the only African admitted to the French Academy; his was some of the best poetry written in French. His socialist party, Union Progressiste Sénégalaise (Senegalese Progressive Union, or UPS), held power from before full independence in 1960 until the elections of 2000. In 1966, the UPS became the country's only political party, and Senghor was reelected overwhelmingly in 1968 and 1973. In 1978, the government mandated a three-party system based on official ideological categories (a fourth party was legalized in 1979).

Along with French culture, Senegal inherited old French bureaucratic centralism and new third-world socialism. This organization and this ideology prevailed throughout the 1970s, where central government ran nearly every institution in the country. Senegal was failing to develop economically, however. State-owned businesses were overstaffed, technologically behind, heavily subsidized, and not performing well.

At the end of 1980, after 24 years in power, Senghor stepped down as president. Abdou Diouf, a member of Senghor's political party, replaced him. Senghor retired to France with his French wife.

Léopold Sédar Senghor is the "Founding Father of Senegal." This photograph was taken on the occasion of his admission to the French Academy in Paris, France, on December 16, 1969.

AFTER SENGHOR

Abdou Diouf became president in 1981 and began a process of political decentralization and an economic move toward a market economy. The 1994 devaluation of Senegal's currency was a major turning point. After successful intervention in a coup attempt in the Gambia, both Senegal and the Gambia officially proclaimed their union in a Senegambian confederation.

In the mid-1980s, deteriorating economic conditions led the government to adopt unpopular austerity measures, causing unrest in both rural and urban areas. Diouf was reelected in the elections of 1988, but two diplomatic crises arose in 1989. First there was a maritime (sea) border dispute with Guinea-Bissau (later resolved by the International Court of Justice in the Netherlands in favor of Senegal) and a violent dispute with Mauritania. In the same year, the confederation with the Gambia dissolved. Also, from 1984 through the 1990s, secessionists from the Casamance fought the Dakar government for the right to form an independent nation. Casamance separatists have long blamed Dakar for economic neglect, lack of job opportunities, land rights issues, and disrespect of cultural norms.

War and Military Intervention

In 1989, a minor incident over grazing rights on the Senegal-Mauritania border led to riots in both countries in which many people died. The countries deported thousands of each other's nationals, killing hundreds in the process. The border was closed, and diplomatic relations were broken off until April 1992. Relations between Senegal and Mauritania remain strained.

In the early 1990s, there were serious clashes between the army and separatist rebels in the Casamance region. The fighting affected Senegal's tourist industry and caused much suffering for the local people. More violence occurred in Casamance and elsewhere in early 1993, after elections in which Diouf was elected president for a third term. After long negotiations, a cease-fire was declared and peace returned to Casamance. By early 1994, tourists had begun to return.

THE TWENTY-FIRST CENTURY

The March 2000 presidential elections were a close contest between President Abdou Diouf and Abdoulaye Wade, leader of the Partie Démocratique Sénégalaise (Senegalese Democratic Party, or PDS). After a tense second round of voting, Wade emerged victorious and is now Senegal's president. This election ended nearly 40 years of Socialist rule in Senegal. Apart from the economy, the most pressing domestic problem for the PDS government is the continuing strife in the Casamance.

4

People
and Culture

Senegal is made up of diverse ethnicities, each of which has helped shape the country's cultural traditions through language, religion, social customs, music, and dance.

POPULATION AND SETTLEMENT

The population of Senegal is estimated at about 10,600,000, with an annual growth rate of 2.6 percent. Young people are the majority of the population: Almost 44 percent of the people in Senegal are under the age of 14.

The overall population density is 143 persons per square mile (55 per square kilometer). The population is not evenly distributed: 65 percent is concentrated on 14 percent of the national territory. More than 60 percent of the population lives in rural settings. The greatest number of people, however, about 23 percent of the total population, is found along the western coast in the

Dakar area, in part because the many administrative, industrial, socioeconomic, and academic facilities there attract and concentrate the population. Rapid urbanization occurring in the Dakar and surroundings areas has stretched social services to their limits and has resulted in urban poverty.

ETHNIC GROUPS

The population of modern Senegal is composed of about a dozen ethnic groups. Most of the groups are closely associated and share many customs, and so a high level of tolerance generally characterizes ethnic relations. There are two recent exceptions to the general environment of ethnic harmony: an ongoing struggle for autonomy by the Diola in Casamance and, from 1989 to 1993, a series of violent attacks on the white Moors living in Senegal. The attacks on the Moors were in retaliation for vicious attacks on blacks in Mauritania, which erupted from a single dispute over a single grazing camel! Most Moors left Senegal after hundreds were killed.

The Wolof is by far the largest and the dominant ethnic group, making up 43 percent of the population. The Wolof are thought to have originated in southern Mauritania and to have moved south because of drought and desert raids. Wolof communities are found from the Senegal River in the north to the Gambia River in the south. They are most highly concentrated in the center of the country, on the north coast between Dakar and Saint-Louis.

Ethnic groups with significant but smaller numbers are the Serer, Pular speakers (mainly Peul and Toucouleur), Mandinke, and Diola. The Serer make up about 14.7 percent of the present population. Originally, they lived in the Senegal River Valley, but between the tenth and the thirteenth centuries, they established themselves in the Baol, a region east of Dakar, along the Petit Côte (Small Coast), and the Sine Saloum area, between Dakar and Kaolack.

Pular speakers account for about 23.8 percent of the population. The Peul, also known as Fulani, Fulbe, and Fula, are a pastoral group that once inhabited the western Sahara. During years of drought, they moved southward to the Senegal River Valley in search of grazing lands. Traditionally nomadic, they are found throughout the Sahel zone and today inhabit the Ferlo, the middle valley of the Senegal River, and the upper Casamance region. Toucouleur (or Haalpular'en as they call themselves) are linguistically related to Peul. They live primarily in the middle part of the Senegal River Valley in northern Senegal and traditionally are farmers, raising both field crops and cattle.

Other smaller ethnic groups include the Lebou, Soninke, and Bassari. The Lebou are a subgroup of Wolof who number about 80,000 persons. They live mainly on the Cap Vert peninsula and along the coast from Kayar to Mbour. Soninke, or Sarakole, who number about one percent of the population, are found in the middle Senegal River Valley between Matam and Bakel. The Bassari live in uplands of southeastern Senegal.

About 105,000 Europeans (mostly French) and Lebanese (one percent) reside in Senegal, mainly in the cities. The remaining population is made up of a number of small indigenous groups as well as immigrants, refugees, and those seeking asylum from other countries including Mauritania, Sierra Leone, Liberia, and Rwanda.

Wolof Ethnic Population

The Wolof formed the core of the Diolof Empire (between A.D. 1200 and 1530). Peanut cultivation became a major occupation during the colonial period, especially among small farmers under the tutelage of the powerful Mourides brotherhood. Many Wolof have settled in cities and work as merchants, in teaching positions, as civil servants, and as skilled craftsmen, but most still live in rural areas and work as subsistence farmers. The Wolof have a highly stratified social system made up of three main castes: freeborn, those of slave descent, and the artisans. This system is somewhat modified in the towns.

The Wolof is the largest and most dominant ethnic group, making up 43 percent of the population. The Wolof are a dark-skinned, tall, proud, and regal-looking people. They are the largest segment of the population in major cities such as Dakar, Saint-Louis, and Kaolack.

Status and Wealth among the Wolof

Status is determined by birth. At the top of the social order are traditional noble and warrior families, followed by the farmers, traders, and persons of caste—artisans such as blacksmiths, leatherworkers, woodworkers, weavers, and *griots*. Griots are of a low caste but are highly respected because they are in charge of passing on the oral traditions and are usually the only ones who can recite a family or village history. Slaves occupied the lowest rung of the social ladder.

They were ethnically diverse people taken in wars and raids, bought, or born into slavery. Slavery is now gone, but many descendants of former slaves still work as tenant farmers for their ancestors' masters.

There are several indicators of wealth in Wolof society. First is the number of wives a man has. The Wolof men generally have from one to four wives, although only the wealthy can afford to have more than one wife. The second indicator is the possession of durable luxury goods including metal beds, bicycles, motorcycles, sewing machines, and modern sporting guns. Only rich farmers own mud-brick or blockhouses. They also have their own plots of land, on which they grow mainly peanuts, but also vegetables and herbs.

Wolof Membership in Islamic Brotherhoods

Islam is an integral part of Wolof culture, although Wolof society is much freer than most Muslim peoples. Women are permitted to appear in public, for example. One important feature of Wolof Islam is that it tends to be centered on membership in one of the three main brotherhoods. About 30 percent of Wolofs belong to the Mourides, about 60 percent belong to the Tijanes, and about 10 percent belong to the Qadiriyas.

WOLOF CHARACTERISTICS AND OCCUPATIONS

The Wolof people are a dark-skinned, tall, proud, regal-looking people. The Wolof have been more affected by the West than other Senegalese groups, yet they have the most highly developed sense of national identity of any Senegalese people. Through the years, the Wolof have played a major role in the import-export trade as middlemen and primary producers of the main cash crop, peanuts. They tend to be a major element of the civil service and play an important part in political parties. They are the largest segment of the population in Senegal's major cities (Dakar, Saint-Louis, Thiès, and

Kaolack). In urban areas, they may be working in businesses such as fabrics, dressmaking, dyeing, jewelry making, and elaborate hairdressing and as teachers and civil servants. In rural areas, they work as subsistence farmers.

Through time, the Wolof have absorbed many traits from other cultures. Language is one such element. An important characteristic of the Wolof is their capacity to influence the ways of others and to adapt to changing situations and yet remain a distinct culture. Other groups admire them for their initiative and ability to adapt. Both the Serer and the Lebou have undergone *Wolofization*, having been somewhat overwhelmed by Wolof culture.

Serer

The Serer are the second-largest ethnic group in Senegal and are a major group in the Gambia. The Kingdom of Sine and Saloum is one of their traditional kingdoms. The Serer have an elaborate religion involving a universal god, called Roog; various dimensions of life and death; space and time; and negotiations with deceased ancestors. They were resistant and slow to adopt Islam, and many Serer areas are now Catholic. The most famous Serer, Senegal's first president, Léopold Sédar Senghor, was Catholic. As the second-largest group in Senegal, they have been somewhat overwhelmed by the dominant Wolof ethnic group. Most Serer speak Wolof as a second language, and, if they have moved to the city, often as a first language.

Pular Speakers and Mandinke

There are five different groups that speak variations of the Pular language. They are the Peul of Walo, from outside of Saint-Louis to the Dagana area; Fulakunda of the Casamance; Fula, from the Fouta Djallon mountains in Guinea; the Laobe, who are a caste of their own; and the Toucouleur of the Fouta Toro.

The two largest groups of Pular speakers are Peul and Toucouleur. The Peul are traditionally a nomadic people who herd cattle, goats, and sheep across the vast, dry hinterlands of their domain, keeping somewhat separate from the local agricultural populations. Today, they are the only major migrating people of West Africa.

The majority of the Toucouleur people occupies a 217-mile-long (350-kilometer-long) and 12-mile-wide (20-kilometer-wide) belt of land along the Senegal River in the Fouta region. Traditionally, Toucouleur have had land and villages on both sides of the Senegal River. Many of the Toucouleur were expelled from Mauritania during the unrest of 1989 and have settled on Senegal's side of the river.

Toucouleur are mostly crop farmers, but they also have become merchants, government officials, and intellectuals. Toucouleur society revolves around two main forces: the clan, subdivided into lineage groups (a kind of family), and the caste system. Toucouleur always gather around a chief, usually an elder or leader of a village, suburb, town, or region. High status is attached to membership in a noble lineage, prosperous family, or leadership in the three major Muslim brotherhoods.

Mandinke society has three divisions: freeborn, artisans, and slaves. The Mandinka are farmers whose main crops are groundnuts, rice, millet, and sorghum. Mandinke society is patrilineal (male-dominated); its smallest social unit is the family. Mandinke are the majority group living in the Gambia.

Diola

Diola were some of the earliest settlers south of the Gambia River. Fiercely independent, the Diola resisted the French influence and today harbor strong separatist feelings. The Diola live in small clan-aligned villages along the Casamance River and are remarkable for their ability to grow mangrove rice.

Diola are very different from other Senegalese. They are one of the few ethnic groups that do not speak Wolof or French.

They are not Muslim; instead, traditional religious beliefs prevail. The majority of Diola, 60 percent, are animist, practicing a religion based on belief in local spirits. During recent decades, about 40 percent have converted to Christianity.

Compared with other groups, Diola society is not organized from the top down. It is egalitarian, with no inferior castes or races. At the village level, a council of clan elders makes all the day-to-day decisions. Important economic activities include the cultivation of wet rice and groundnuts and production of palm wine.

Lebou, Soninke, and Bassari

The Lebou are primarily a fishing community, although they also are employed in the construction trades. Most of the market women in Dakar are Lebou, but they speak Wolof. The Lebou political and spiritual capital is at Yoff, just north of Dakar. Other Lebou centers are Oakam and Ngor.

Lebou society emphasizes piety and respect for elders, and Lebou families include not only living people but also associated ancestral spirits. The Lebou are noted for their public exorcism dances and rituals, which tourists often attend.

Soninke are farmers and traders and are known as industrious people. After the harvest, many younger people move to neighboring countries to look for work. The women busy themselves at home with crafts, including producing and dyeing material. Dark blue indigo is considered a typical Soninke color. Many Soninke now live in France—mostly in Paris but also in other industrial areas—where they often work in the automobile industry. With the men gone, Soninke villages are primarily peopled by women, children, and the very old.

The Bassari are a small group living in the hills and mesas of southeastern Senegal. Over centuries, their clans were raided for slaves. Today, in their rather isolated location, they maintain their traditional way of life more than do most groups. They raise millet and corn but also hunt and gather.

The Bassari are a small group that lives in the hills and mesas of southeastern Senegal. Their rather isolated location has allowed them to maintain a traditional way of life that includes agriculture, hunting, and gathering.

LANGUAGE

From 1895 to 1958, Senegal was a French colony. When it became an independent nation, French was adopted as the official language. Only the literate minority use French regularly, however; all Senegalese speak an indigenous (native) language. There are 36 different languages spoken in Senegal, of which Wolof has the greatest usage. Wolof and six other prominent African tongues—Jola-Fogny, Malinke, Mandinke, Pular, Serer-Sine, and Soninke—have been made "national languages"; this status allows them to be used in schools. Arabic expressions also are common in Senegalese speech.

The Wolof language is the lingua franca (common language) of Senegal, especially in urban areas. The Wolof people are the ethnic majority in the country, and some members of other ethnic groups have adopted Wolof as their native language. More than half of the remaining population uses Wolof as a second or third language. These three groups of Wolof-speakers account for about 80 of the population, making Senegal one of the most linguistically unified countries in West Africa.

RELIGION

More than 94 percent of Senegal's population, including the Wolof, Toucouleur, and Mandinke, is Muslim. The rest of the population is made up of 4 percent animists and 2 percent Christian. The Peul and the Diola are animists by tradition, whereas many of the Serer are Catholic.

Islam

The style of Islam practiced in Senegal is significantly different from that in most other Islamic countries. Senegalese are Sunni Muslims and Sufi followers. Sufis practice Islam in a mystic way, following the basic tenets of Islam but not all of the orthodox practices. In Senegal, it is a movement of organized brotherhoods that follow charismatic religious leaders (marabouts) or sheiks.

More than 94 percent of the Senegalese population is Muslim. These Muslims are praying on a beach outside Dakar at the start of the holiday of Tabaski. The celebration of Tabaski entails the sacrifice of a sheep or a goat and commemorates the biblical story of Abraham, who was ready to sacrifice his son when God interceded by substituting a ram in the child's place.

Virtually all Senegalese belong to one of four brotherhoods or orders: the Mourides, the Tijanes (Tidianes), the Qadiriyya (Xaadir, Khadirs), and the Layenes. These orders are a powerful influence in Senegalese life and politics. Belonging to a brotherhood is passed down through the family. Few people would think of making a big decision without consulting their town's grand marabout. During the colonial period, the brotherhoods were the main means by which the Sufi form of Islam was spread. Since Senegal won independence, Islam has become the primary force in Senegalese society due to the brotherhoods' ability to adapt to changing social conditions, including the spread of Koranic primary schools and Senegal's growing political ties with the Islamic world.

Muslim Brotherhoods

The Qadiriyya brotherhood is the oldest. It was founded by the Sufi mystic Abdul Qadir al-Jilani in the twelfth century and spread to Senegal in the eighteenth century. It is now pan-Islamic. The Tijanes, the largest brotherhood in membership, represents approximately half of the population. The Mourides, the richest of the brotherhoods, is gaining in popularity, especially among younger people. It has more than one million members, many of whom live in the urban areas. The real core of the Mouride movement is in agricultural areas, especially the groundnut-growing region. Its expansion toward the southern part of the country is coincident with the spread of groundnut cultivation.

The Layene order is a religious sect of the Lebou people. The Tijanes order was founded by the Algerian marabout Al-Tijaniyya, who called himself a "prophet of Al'lah." The Tijanes are far stricter in their observance of rites than are members of other Sufi orders.

Amadou Bamba M'Backé established Mouridism as an offshoot of Qadiriyya in late nineteenth century, at a time when French influence was growing. His teachings emphasize hard physical work and clean living and require unquestioned devotion to the marabout, as well as the standard religious observances of Islam. Amadou Bamba was headquartered at Touba, where the largest mosque in Senegal, and perhaps the largest in sub-Saharan Africa, stands. The Great Mosque at Touba is a destination point for religious pilgrimages. Amadou

Bamba is attributed with extraordinary powers. Stories about his trials at the hands of the French and his miraculous escapes abound. He is said to have been imprisoned in a cell with a hungry lion, cast into a fiery furnace, buried for seven days in a deep well, and kept on an island inhabited by snakes and devils. One of the most popular legends is about his voyage of exile to Gabon. When a captain refused him permission to pray, Bamba jumped overboard and laid his prayer mat on the ocean floor to pray in peace.

Christianity

Christians, mostly Roman Catholic, number about 565,000. Catholicism was introduced in the country first by Portuguese missionaries in the Casamance and then by French priests. Less than one percent of the population is Protestant. Most Protestants are members of Assemblies of God, Worldwide Evangelization for Christ, and related evangelical churches.

Animism

Animist beliefs prevail among the Diola of the lower Casamance and several other remote groups. Classic animism attributes conscious life to natural objects or phenomena.

Traditional Beliefs, Practices, and Taboos

Despite the strong Islamic and to a lesser extent Christian influences in Senegal today, many people retain practices that originated in past animist beliefs. Many Senegalese people wear amulets (called "gris gris") around their waists, necks, arms, or legs. Gris gris are leather pouches with enclosed writings from the Koran, which have been prescribed by a marabout.

Senegalese people consult religious authorities called marabouts for a variety of reasons, usually to protect against evil spirits, improve status (in getting a job, seeking love or marriage, or getting a promotion), remedy a situation (curing a mentally or physically ill person, treating headaches or chronic pains, or resolving disputes between people), and curse (eliminating a rival through illness, disappearance, or death).

CLASS STRUCTURE

Despite the changes brought on by urbanization and modernization, Senegalese society still is influenced by the class structure of its past. A rigid social stratification traditionally characterized all major Senegalese ethnic groups except the Diola. Wolof, Serer, and Toucouleur societies are organized according to two systems: caste and order. The caste system is aligned closely with the division of labor, and the order is associated with political power. The segregation of castes intervenes most significantly at the level of marriage. Marriages between castes or between nobles and lower castes are problematic. Those that do occur usually are among urban people whose positions of social privilege are a result of money, political power, or religion.

Traditional Music

Musical activity in Senegal often is related to caste structure. By tradition, music making belongs to a social class of griots who are considered to be of a lower caste. The higher castes are content to be entertained. Griots are divided into two groups: those who are musicians and sing the praises of a family and those who speak and at the same time have the right to threaten, abuse, and mock rich persons. As the lowest of all the castes, they are feared and despised but also valued for their knowledge of family history.

Griot families were attached to noble families, from which they received protection and generous remuneration in exchange for their services. Until the colonial period, however, griots had to live in segregated sections of villages. Sometimes they were denied underground burial and instead were buried in hollow baobab trees. Today, such discrimination is illegal and the worst prejudices and superstitions are suppressed. In the nineteenth century, religious wars and colonial influence caused the breakup of ruling noble families. Many griots were forced to adopt several patrons, and others became freelance musicians. The griot's new occupation became entertainer and musician instead of genealogist and historian.

Modern griots travel constantly in pursuit of someone who is able to pay for entertainment. Griots appear regularly at weddings, naming ceremonies, and other special occasions attended by their traditional patron. Many have become successful as musicians and singers on the international scene. In the religious society, they specialize as *muezzins* (announcers of prayer) and in religious chants.

Musical Instruments

Many types of musical instruments are found in Senegal, most made by griots. All the instruments, whether string, percussion, or wind, are made from native materials such as gourds, animal skins, millet stalks, or horn.

Sabar, a type of drum, is the most common instrument. Almost all sabar drumming is accompanied by dancing and usually takes place on special occasions and festivals including births, naming ceremonies, weddings, holidays, and other special celebrations. The sabar has become the backbone of almost every Senegalese music group.

The *tama*, nearly as common as the sabar, is played by Wolof, Serer, Peul, Toucouleur, and Mandinke musicians. The tama is a "talking drum," or a drum whose pitch can be regulated.

The *kora* is often called the African harp. Although it originated in the Gambia River Valley with the Mandinke, it is one of the most popular instruments in Senegal. It is made from half of a large gourd covered with goatskin stretched tight with metal tacks. Most koras have 21 strings, but they may have as many as 25 strings.

DANCE

Dynamic and rhythmic dances, the most popular of which is called *mbalax*, are performed at many celebrations. There are other special dances performed during wrestling matches, on holidays, and on other occasions.

Although each ethnic group has its favorite drumming tunes and unique dance styles, most Senegalese perform a similar popular dance. A semicircle or full circle is formed with the dancers facing the drummers, and one by one, dancers come forward for a short but spirited display of footwork and vigorous hip movements.

5

Administration and Government

Senegal is a democratic country known for its stable government and ability to change leadership in a peaceful manner. This chapter describes and explains how Senegal is governed and administratively divided and what problems it faces as an emerging African nation. It also examines the country's transportation, communication, education, and health care.

ADMINISTRATIVE REGIONS

Senegal is administered centrally from Dakar. Administrative divisions are composed of a hierarchal arrangement of 11 regions, 34 departments, and 93 districts called *arrondissements*. Regions take their names from their capital cities. The 11 regions and their departments are as follows:

- Region of Dakar: area, 212 square miles (550 square kilometers);

capital, Dakar; made up of the departments of Dakar, Guediawaye, Pikine, and Rufisque

- Region of Diourbel: area, 1,722 square miles (4,459 square kilometers); capital, Diourbel; includes the departments of Bambey, Diourbel, and Mbacke

- Region of Fatick: area, 3,064 square miles (7,935 square kilometers); capital, Fatick; contains the departments of Fatick, Foundiougne, and Gossas

- Region of Kaolack: area, 6,181.5 square miles (16,010 square kilometers); capital, Kaolack; comprises the departments of Kaffrine, Kaolack, and Nioro du Rip

- Region of Kolda: area, 8,112 square miles (21,011 square kilometers); capital; Kolda; includes the departments of Kolda, Sedhiou, and Velingara

- Region of Louga: area, 11,269.5 square miles (29,188 square kilometers); capital, Louga; made up of the departments of Kebemer, Linguere, and Louga

- Region of Matam: area, 9,684.6 square miles (25,083 square kilometers); capital, Matam; comprises the departments of Kanel, Matam, and Ranerou Ferlo

- Region of Saint-Louis: area, 7,353 square miles (19,044 square kilometers); capital, Saint-Louis; includes the departments of Dagana, Podor, and Saint-Louis

- Region of Tambacounda: area, 23,012.5 square miles (59,602 square kilometers); capital, Tambacounda; contains the departments of Bakel, Kedougou, and Tambacounda

- Region of Thiès: area, 2,549 square miles (6,601 square kilometers); capital, Thiès; includes the departments of Mbour, Thiès, and Tivaouane

- Region of Ziguinchor: area, 2,988 square miles (7,739 square kilometers); capital, Ziguinchor; made up of the departments of Bignona, Oussouye, and Ziguinchor

GOVERNMENT

Senegal is a republic governed under multiparty democratic rule. It is moderately decentralized (some governmental functions are handled by local authorities and institutions) and dominated by a strong presidency. Currently, the government operates under the constitution of 2001. The president, who is the chief of state, is directly elected to a five-year term. A prime minister, appointed by the president, is the head of state. The prime minister, in consultation with the president, appoints a council of ministers.

The legislative power is a 120-seat, single-house national assembly (Assemblée Nationale). Assembly members are elected to five-year terms of office, and voting is open to all citizens 18 years and older. The legal system is based on French civil law, with judicial review of legislative acts in the Constitutional Court. Other arms of the judiciary are the Council of State, Court of Appeals, and the Court of Final Appeals.

After the 2000 election, the government underwent a major change in leadership policies, with a pronounced shift toward decentralization. From 1960 until 2000, the Parti Socialiste Senegalais (PSS) monopolized national politics. Although Senegal was never formally a one-party state, Léopold Sédar Senghor of the PSS remained president from 1960 to 1981. In 2000, opposition leader Abdoulaye Wade of the Senegalese Democratic Party (PDS), backed by a coalition of other opposition parties, became president in an election judged to be free and fair. The postelection transition period was free of violence and characterized by good conduct on the part of all candidates. In local elections held in 2000, President Wade's coalition gained control of the majority of rural, regional, and city councils. The government continued to implement decentralized regional and local administrations. In a January 2001 referendum, 94 percent of voters accepted a new constitution, which abolished the Senate, a body that had no directly elected members.

In 2000, Abdoulaye Wade of the Senegalese Democratic Party was elected president in an election judged to be free and fair.

PORTS, AIRPORTS, RAILS, AND ROADS

Senegal's transportation system is inadequate. Since winning independence, Senegal has done little to maintain or upgrade the transportation infrastructure left by the French. Roads and, especially railroads, have fallen into disrepair. A relatively new Transport Sector Adjustment Program (PAST), largely funded by the World Bank and smaller international entities, is putting $600 million into transportation programs. Most of this money is going toward highways, including repaving and extending the three main roads radiating outward from Dakar. The country's road network, although largely unpaved surfaces, is relatively good. Only about one-third of Senegal's 9,700 miles (14,600 kilometers) of roads are paved.

Senegal's highway network includes three primary routes: a central route from Dakar to the border with Mali, the northern route to Mauritania, and the southern route that extends toward the Gambia and Casamance region. Currently, two major roads, the road leading from Dakar to Ziguinchor in southern Senegal via Kaolack and the road from Tambacounda north to Ourossogui on the Mauritania border, are being upgraded. The west-central part of Senegal, which includes the communities of Saint-Louis, Louga, Dakar, Thiès, and Kaolack, is especially well connected by roads.

Traffic congestion is a major problem in and around Dakar. Parking in Dakar is nearly impossible, and the fine for parking illegally is $11, a relatively large amount of money. Brightly painted minibuses and vans are the main means of transportation for most Senegalese living the Dakar metropolitan area. Taxis are everywhere, and "bush" taxis take passengers to and from Dakar and the regional capitals and, on request, will stop at smaller towns and villages.

Rail service extends north and east of Dakar and consists of about 560 miles (900 kilometers) of track. The railroad running north from Dakar to Saint-Louis transports freight only. The only passenger line extends east, linking Dakar and Bamako (in Mali) with weekly service. The train to Bamako is a major carrier of freight, passengers, and baggage on its journey, which takes 24 to 36 hours. Small traders, mostly women, also ride the trains. They crowd everywhere—empty freight cars, hallways, spaces between cars, and even bathrooms. There is usually a major delay at the border as engines are switched (the one line is run by two companies) and customs of both countries are cleared.

Dakar is the country's leading port and also has an international airport. Ports and harbors include Dakar, Kaolack, Matam, Podor, Richard Toll, Saint-Louis, and Ziguinchor. River traffic is negligible. Air transport is well developed within the country and serves 15 cities besides Dakar. Competition from roads has reduced transportation by sea and rail to the north. To the south, however, the road has two border crossings at the Gambia, making boat travel competitively priced from Dakar to Ziguinchor, the Casamance port. Several international carriers, including Air Afrique and Air France, serve Dakar. Air Senegal, a state-owned company with two airplanes, has a monopoly on national flights.

COMMUNICATION

Senegal benefits from modern communication technology. Although it has only one government television station, the country receives many French stations via satellite. Many urban Senegalese have televisions, and broadcasts of the 10 AM and 14 FM radio stations reach much of the country. In 2003, there was one phone company in Senegal that provided service to 280,000 customers. Cell phone users number around 700,000, and that number is growing rapidly.

In terms of phone usage, there is a huge gap between Dakar and the rest of the country. Sixty percent of the main phone lines are concentrated in Dakar, as are 80 percent of the cell phone users. Personal computer ownership is growing, and the city now has four Internet service providers. Between 2000 and 2001 alone, the number of Internet users in Senegal increased 150 percent, and Senegal ranks as one of Africa's leading users of Internet services. In April 2002, Senegal counted 12,000 Internet subscribers, but roughly 100,000 Senegalese were active users and regularly connected in the 150 access points such as cyber cafés and phone centers.

In underdeveloped countries, cyber cafés are the main means for connecting to the Internet, and Senegal is no exception. This avoids the hassle and cost of buying a computer, finding an Internet provider, waiting for hookup, and the expensive monthly charges.

EDUCATION

Education receives 33 percent of the national budget. It is compulsory for children ages 6 to 13, but actual enrollment in primary school is only 56 percent of the school-age population (67 percent boys and 56 percent girls). The illiteracy rate in Senegal is an astounding 67 percent of the population older than 15 years of age. (Illiteracy in Africa as a whole is about 42 percent.) In the more remote regions of the country, the rates have climbed to a staggering 80 percent, and those for girls and women are even higher.

In 2000, Senegal had fallen far behind in the education of its children, even by African standards. Critics point to a lack of schools, few well-trained teachers, and inadequate teaching materials. The state-run school system also hinders innovation and change.

Few children who attend school stay for more than a couple of years. Many forces combine to spell an early end to education, especially for girls. Chief among them is poverty. The cost of voluntary contributions, uniforms, books, and bus fares can make even free education expensive, especially if there are many children in a family. The daughters usually are withdrawn from school. In a poor family, a daughter can help in cleaning, cooking, collecting wood and water, and looking after younger children. Even if she is educated, there will be little opportunity for her to get a paying job.

Quality education is available to wealthy Senegalese living in cities. Education in Senegal has two competing sectors: traditional education and modern education. Traditional education requires children to be instructed in the Koran and Arabic at an early age so they can be good Muslims. A significant percentage of school-age children attend these schools, so the

Senegal has fallen far behind in the education of its children. Few children who attend school stay for more than a few years. This classroom may be the setting for a free education, but supplies, bus fares, and books, combined with the loss of the children's help in the home encourage them to leave schooling early.

schools receive some government funding. Today, they are declining in importance, however, because of competition from the French, or the modern school.

Since independence, the government has supported modern education. As an incentive civil servants who send their children to French schools receive a special allowance. The Senegalese education system is inherited from the French. Its system goes from kindergarten through university level. Kindergarten is private and is an optional three-year program; it starts at the age of two or three and ends at the age of five or six, depending on the child's performance. Often, Koranic schooling takes the place of French-style kindergartens.

Primary or elementary school lasts six years and ends with a competitive exam that screens those who wish to go to middle school or "college." "College" is a three-year program that also ends with a selective exam. Those who pass receive a diploma. Students must score of 10 out of 20 to get into the lycée (high school). They then spend three years in the lycée and finish with the baccalaureate.

Higher education recently underwent some changes. The baccalaureate is no longer an automatic passport to university studies, and different schools have different enrollment standards. Senegal has two public universities, two private ones, and several technical or professional schools. Public universities are the University of Cheikh Anta Diop in Dakar and Gaston Berger University in Saint-Louis.

French is Senegal's official language and the one used in the schools. Students start learning English in their first year of "college" (at the age of 12) and they must also study another foreign language such as Spanish, Russian, German, and Arabic.

The typical school day goes from 8:00 A.M. to 12:00 P.M. and from 3:00 P.M. to 5:00 P.M. on Monday, Tuesday, Thursday, and Friday. Students have a three-hour break to go home, eat with the family, and rest, and then they go back to school. No classes are held Wednesday afternoons or on weekends. There are no commencement ceremonies in the French based-system.

HEALTH CARE

In Senegal, life expectancy is not especially high, averaging only about 56 years (54.3 for males and 57.3 for females). Healthy life expectancy is even lower. Like many others living in sub-Saharan Africa, Senegalese live with chronic disease. Government and international aid programs are at work in Senegal to improve health care and to mitigate and, where possible, eliminate disease. Infant mortality, though still high, has declined by 50 percent during the past 25 years.

High birth rates are common in countries with high infant mortality, and Senegal is no exception: The birth rate for 2003 was 36.23 births per 1,000.

Health System

During the past 20 years, Senegal's health system has moved from a program that emphasized curative care to treat patients for disease to one that stresses primary health care (which includes check-ups and dietary advice) and community participation. A network of 750 health posts and about 8,000 Village Health Workers (VHWs) form the base of the health care system. Nurses who staff the health posts are the key health providers. They are responsible for a variety of curative and preventive services, including supervision and in-service training of the VHWs, health and nutrition education, and record keeping.

Problems that cannot be resolved at the village or health post level are referred to the 52 health centers. These posts are the first level of referral and are usually located in the district capital. One or two medical doctors manage the health centers, which are designed to provide outpatient, limited inpatient service, and laboratory services and to supervise the health posts. Hospitals are located in the regional capitals and are the second level in the referral system. With the exception of the Kolda and Fatick, each region has a regional hospital staffed with medical teams.

Common Diseases

Infectious diseases are the main cause of chronic illness and death in Senegal. Malaria, respiratory infections, and diarrhea are the most prevalent types of illness. In recent years, there has been a decrease in epidemic diseases such as cholera, but endemic (native) diseases such as malaria, schistosomiasis, onchocerciasis, and hepatitis B have increased. A new scourge is the emergence of the viral diseases such as AIDS. Besides

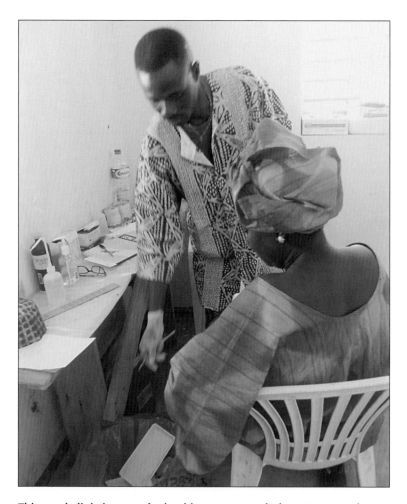

This rural clinic is part of a health care network that stresses primary health care and community participation. Problems that cannot be resolved at the local level are referred to 52 health centers that are usually located in one of the 93 district capitals.

infectious disease, tuberculosis and periodic yellow fever outbreaks plague the country.

In Senegal, malaria is a chronic disease, accounting for 40 to 50 percent of visits to health clinics; it is one of the main causes of death and a major burden on society. Malaria is responsible for high mortality in children from six months to five years of age (about 25 percent of all deaths in these groups) who have not yet developed immunity to the disease. The cost of treating malaria is one percent of the gross domestic product (GDP) in Senegal (about U.S. $6 million). Senegal is actively participating in the Roll Back Malaria Partnership (RBM). The World Health Organization (WHO) began this international effort in 1998 with the goal of reducing the world's malaria burden by half by 2010.

Statistically, schistosomiasis is a relatively minor disease in Senegal, but the development of agricultural and irrigation projects has led to environmental changes that encourage the spread of the disease. During recent years, intestinal schistosomiasis outbreaks have reached epidemic proportions in the Saint-Louis region.

Senegal is considered one of the developing world's success stories in HIV prevention. It has maintained one of the lowest HIV prevalence levels in sub-Saharan Africa, and HIV1 prevalence has stabilized since 1997. The estimated number of adults and children living with HIV and AIDS is 70,000, out of a total population of about 9.7 million.

6

Economy

By most standards, Senegal is classed as a less-developed country (LDC). It has a long way to go to achieve the level of economic prosperity enjoyed by industrial nations. Senegal faces many economic problems that hinder economic growth, but even so, it is better off than many other African countries.

Since the country won independence in 1960, the Senegalese economy has seen contrasting developments. The first five years were characterized by high growth. By the late 1970s and through the 1980s, the economy was stagnant (unchanging). In 1993, Senegal plunged into a serious economic crisis. A bold plan of economic reform was put into place in 1995, and, as a result, the economy now is experiencing strong economic growth. Much of the country's economic activity follows tradition: In the countryside, most people are involved in raising crops or livestock or fishing, and rural poverty is common.

ECONOMIC WEALTH

What is the wealth and economic potential of Senegal? Gross domestic product (GDP) is one of a number of measures used to determine the wealth and health of the economy of a country. GDP is defined as the market value of all property and goods produced by labor within a country. During the early years of the twenty-first century, Senegal's GDP amounted to about (U.S.) $4.9 billion. Of the different sectors, agriculture contributed 18 percent, industry 27 percent, and services 55 percent. When converted to purchasing power parity (PPP)—its equivalent to purchasing power in the United States—Senegal's GDP was estimated at about (U.S.) $16.2 billion (2002). By this measure, Senegal is one of the world's poorer countries. According to the United Nations Human Development Index, it is ranked 145 out of 162 countries. This ranking is slightly higher than its neighbors Burkina Faso (159) and Guinea (150) but lower than its northern neighbor, Mauritania (139). Approximately 54 percent of the population is below the poverty line. In 2002, GDP per capita PPP was estimated at about U.S. $1,500, but this excludes a large informal economy, which is not measured easily.

Since the devaluation of the Communauté Financière Africaine (African Financial Community, or CFA) franc in 1994, the government has implemented a series of economic policy reforms that have promoted economic growth. Devaluation is a decrease in value of a country's currency relative to the that of other countries. GDP per capita has been growing at an average rate of about 5 percent per year since 1995.

Exports account for about one-third of Senegal's GDP. The government receives external assistance from international financial institutions and other sources, which is approximately 32 percent of the national budget. Money sent home from Senegalese living in Europe and the United States represents 3 to 4 percent of the GDP.

Finance and Money

Senegal shares its currency with a group of other former French West African colonies. These countries participate in the CFA, a monetary union. The CFA, which is also the name of the currency, is run by the Banque Centrale des États de l'Afrique de l'Ouest (Central Bank of West African States). One American dollar is equal to about 550 CFA francs.

Unlike most currencies, the CFA does not float, that is, it does not vary in value daily in competition with other currencies. It is tied to the French franc (FF) at a fixed rate. The advantage in this for France-Senegal commerce is the simple, fixed exchange rate. It also is a benefit for West African commerce, helping create a market big enough to grow as a more modern economy.

Unfortunately, over time, the CFA got out of adjustment with FF. In January 1994, France devalued the CFA, cutting the exchange value in half. For 30 years, the rate had been 50 CFA per FF; in an instant, it was 100 CFA per FF. Overnight, all import prices doubled. Just as quickly, Senegal received half the value in foreign currency of everything it sold on world markets. A restructuring program had begun officially 10 years earlier, but the devaluation jolted the process forward.

The immediate result was hardship. Minibus fares rose to cover higher costs of imported gasoline. Inflation hit 30 percent briefly, but more realistic prices led to the current cycle of growth. Inflation currently has dropped below 3.5 percent. Domestic and foreign investments are up, and exports are increasing faster than imports. Senegal's external debt has stabilized, and the system of government price controls and subsidies has been largely dismantled. Since 2002, the euro has replaced the FF as the mother currency of the CFA franc.

Trade

France has traditionally been Senegal's leading trade partner, although Senegal has considerable trade with other European Union (EU) countries, as well as with India, Mali, Nigeria, and Thailand. The chief imports are foodstuffs (especially rice and wheat), machinery, transportation equipment, and crude petroleum.

Rice is Senegal's staple food. Currently, the country must import more than three-quarters of the grain consumed domestically. Many Senegalese rice farmers have difficulty selling their crop, because cheaper rice can be imported from Asia and the Senegalese prefer the broken Asian rice to the long-grain rice grown locally. Thailand and Vietnam are the largest suppliers. Wheat, used mainly in making flour, is second on the list of agricultural imports.

Senegal's exports are mostly commodities (primary goods used in manufacturing) that, unfortunately, are susceptible to changing international prices. Its principal customers are India, France, Spain, Italy, Greece, and Mali. The main exports include peanuts and peanut products, calcium phosphate, processed fish, petroleum products, and cotton. Export earnings from groundnut (peanut) products (oil and groundnut cake) have increased slightly since the CFA devaluation. Fish has replaced the groundnut as Senegal's major export. Industrial fishing operations struggle with high costs, however, and Senegalese tuna is rapidly losing the French market to more efficient Asian competitors. Phosphate production is the third major foreign exchange earner. Exports with smaller earnings are cotton and petroleum products.

ECONOMIC ACTIVITIES

Senegal has a relatively diversified economy. Activities include farming and herding, fishing, forestry, industry, mining, services, and tourism.

Crops

Senegal is primarily an agricultural country, although industry is gaining in the cities, especially Dakar. Agriculture plays an essential role in the national economy and in providing a substantial portion of the nation's food supply. More than 70 percent of Senegal's labor force is engaged in farming, which is largely based on rain-fed (dryland) cultivation.

Peanut production accounts for half of Senegal's agricultural yield. Peanuts generally are grown on small farms in central Senegal between the Sine and Saloum rivers near Diourbel and Kaolack.

Duration and seasonal distribution of precipitation create two different production zones, north and south of the Gambia River. The average farming season lasts three to five months, diminishing from north to south. In the north, sorghum, millet, peas, and peanuts are the main crops. In the south, rice, maize (corn), peanuts, cotton, and sorghum are grown.

Groundnut (peanut) production accounts for half of Senegal's agricultural yield. In a good year, Senegal is the world's leading producer of groundnuts. Although the groundnut's share of total export value has fallen drastically in recent years, it is still a major source of rural income and is critical to one of Senegal's major industries: groundnut oil mills. Groundnuts for the most part are grown on small farms in central Senegal between the Sine and Saloum rivers near Kaolack and Diourbel.

Other cash crops include cotton and market vegetables (tomatoes, squash, and green vegetables). Cotton is a relatively new cash crop that has been planted with some success. About 43 percent of cotton produced is used domestically; the remainder is exported. There also has been a significant expansion in market vegetables.

Most farmers combine cash cropping with planting food crops, the emphasis shifting according to weather patterns. Food crops, especially rice, maize, millet, sorghum, and peas, currently provide about two-thirds of the country's food needs. Sorghum, pearl millet, and cowpeas are grown in the central and Sahelian northern regions. Rice is grown in the floodplains of the Senegal, Saloum, and Casamance rivers and with irrigation in the Senegal River Valley. It is estimated that water for Senegal's harvested rice area is divided equally by recession flooding along riverbanks and controlled irrigation. In the southern Casamance region, rice is produced mainly by recessional irrigation along the floodplains.

With rain-fed (dryland) cultivation, the growing cycle coincides with the short wet season. Choices of crops and places where they are planted are tied closely to the amount, distribution, and timing of rainfall. Crops in the northern half of the country are particularly prone to the effects of erratic rainfall and drought. Farmers in the dry Senegal River Valley practice a combination of farming techniques, including rain-fed (*dieri*), flood recessional (*walo*), valley bottom (*bas-fonds*), controlled recessional, and irrigated agriculture. Despite low rainfall, the valley farmers generally count on two harvests, one dependent on summer rains on sandy upland soils and the other on postsummer floods on the river's alluvial (containing stream-deposited soil) floodplain. Some years, only the irrigated crops produce well.

Flood recession farming is a traditional production method in which planting takes place after floodwaters of the Senegal River recede. This is similar to what was practiced in Egypt before the construction of dams on the Nile River. Land used for recession farming (*walo*) is subdivided into *falo, hollade,* and *fonde.* Falo is practiced on the steep riverbed slopes and is a system in which maize, beans, watermelons, and potatoes are raised. The hollade areas form the bulk of the floodplain and are used for millet, beans, and watermelon. Fonde is practiced on the high ground that is rarely inundated and therefore is only used occasionally. Much has been written about possible negative affects of dam construction on the Senegal River on flood recessional agriculture.

Because of the limited amount of land suitable for crops and the erratic rainfall in much of the country, it is not surprising that the Senegalese government is promoting irrigation as a way of achieving food security. At present, about 3 percent of arable land is irrigated, mostly along the Senegal, Saloum, and Casamance Rivers. One of the larger irrigation projects is the raising of sugarcane at Richard Toll in the Senegal River Valley. This operation, owned by the Senegalese Sugar Company, owes its success to a steady water supply above Diama Dam, located near the mouth of river.

Agriculture Methods

Senegal has 440,000 farms, which are mostly small-scale family operations. The family unit dominates, but, at peak times, villagers help each other. Every adult family member has a plot of land and also works on the farm owned by the head of the family. Cultivation methods are simple, and tools range from the traditional hoe to horse-drawn implements. Usually, fields are burned before the rainy season and the ash fertilizes the crops. There is little use of chemical fertilizers or animal manure, except among the Serer farmers, who do use cattle manure to fertilize their fields.

Market Fruits and Vegetables

Senegal grows a variety of fruits and vegetables and also imports them from Europe. Local farmers grow lettuce, cucumbers, and carrots year round. Senegal exports green beans (French beans), melons, and peppers to the EU and imports apples, oranges, and grapefruits from France and onions and potatoes from the Netherlands. Fruit and vegetable production in the country has risen steadily since 1991, and most produce is sold domestically or within the region.

Vendors sell pineapples, bananas, mangoes, grapefruits, oranges, and palm kernels from the Casamance; mangoes, cashews, watermelons, and mandarin oranges from west central Senegal; and baobab fruit from the central part of the country and the north. Vegetables appearing in the markets include onions, squash, tomatoes, okra, sesame, as well as beans, peppers, lettuce, carrots, and cucumbers.

Livestock

Large numbers of cattle, sheep, and goats are raised in Senegal, although intermittent drought conditions can reduce their populations. An estimated 4.5 million sheep, 3 million cattle, and 3.1 million goats are found in Senegal today. Other livestock include poultry, horses, and pigs, the last raised in non-Muslim sections of the country.

Pastoral nomads, semi-nomads, and sedentary farmers raise livestock in Senegal. Pastoral groups have lived in Senegal for centuries. Nomads, following centuries-old traditions, move their animals seasonally. When the rains cease in one location, the nomads move elsewhere in search of new pasture and watering holes. In Senegal, this search takes them from the savannas of the Ferlo region in the north to more fertile areas in the south, a move that has consequences: With livestock movement, there is a risk of introducing or spreading disease. Moreover, traveling such long distances wears out the already poorly nourished herds, leading to lower milk and meat production.

As pastoralists and farmers meet and compete for the same land and water, conflict often occurs. Pastoralists need open spaces for extensive grazing, but farmers enclose their land to

Large numbers of cattle, sheep, and goats are raised in Senegal, although drought can affect their populations. These long-horned guzera cattle on the plains of the Sahel region live in the most arid part of Senegal. The livestock owners must move these animals in search of new pasture and watering holes.

ensure that animals do not eat or trample crops. Some of the confrontations between farmers and pastoralists have reached alarming proportions. In 1991, thousands of Peul people and more than 100,000 cattle were expelled from the forest reserve of Mbegu to make way for groundnut farmers.

The Peul are a pastoral group that grows a few subsistence crops but lives mostly from the milk and meat of its cattle, sheep, and goats. They are far less mobile now than they were 50 years ago. In the past, herders moved their families out of the Ferlo when the watering holes dried up during the dry season. Then, in the 1950s, the French government began to drill boreholes (wells) 600 to 1,000 feet (200 to 300 meters) into the aquifer. There is now a grid of wells, with pumping stations at about 18-mile (30-kilometer) intervals. The Peul have set up semipermanent camps or villages around the water sources; some cultivate small crops of millet during the rainy season

(July to October). They live by exchanging dairy produce for cereal foods, and rarely kill cattle for meat. Most people remain there year–round, but one or two men accompany the cattle, guiding them from borehole to borehole depending on the availability of water and the quality of pastures. Thus the Peul have become semi-nomads, and some have become permanently settled cattle ranchers.

Surprisingly, the greatest density of cattle is found not in the north where the traditional Peul pastoralists live, but in the west central part of the country and in the Casamance. Among Wolof farmers, cattle are valued as an economic asset. All rich farmers of a village have a herd, generally acquired through inheritance, although the Wolof invest in cattle whenever possible. Some give the cattle to Peul herdsmen to care for; in fact, many Wolof villages have arrangements with Peul herders. Peul cattle are permitted to graze on crop residues and, in return, the cattle are tied up on the land near the village at night to fertilize it with manure.

Cattle stock may be sold for a number of reasons, including to pay for a pilgrimage to Mecca or to gain another wife. Most families keep sheep and goats. These animals usually are owned by women and herded by children. Horses and donkeys have been increasing in number because of their usefulness for pulling farm implements and carts.

Sheep play an important cultural role in Senegal's dominantly Islamic society. Each year, Muslims celebrate the feast of Tabaski (Feast of Sacrifice, or The Great Feast). So many sheep are required for the celebration that live animals must be imported from neighboring countries.

Fishing

Fish long have played a vital role in Senegalese culture, income, and diet, and fishing is an important socioeconomic activity. Senegal's cold coastal waters are rich in fish, although recent overfishing seriously threatens the resources. Flirting teenagers use the name of Senegal's main catch—*thiof*—as a synonym for "cute."

The fishing industry is Senegal's largest source of foreign exchange, making up 30 percent of total exports and about 2.5 percent of the GDP. About 66 percent of Senegal's fish exports go to Europe, and the remainder is traded to the United States and various countries in the region. The Asian market is marginal, although exports of octopus to Japan reached 13,000 tons in 1999. Senegalese fishery exports benefit greatly from an exemption of customs duties in the European market.

Fish is a major part of the Senegalese diet; in fact, spiced fish and rice is the country's national dish. On average, the Senegalese eat more fish than do Americans and almost as much as the French. Unfortunately, it is becoming increasingly difficult to buy fish. Harvests are declining, and more of the catch is being exported because devaluation of the CFA franc has made exporting more lucrative. This caused prices on the domestic market to rise substantially, which means that people either have to pay more for fish or consume less.

Senegal has well-developed coastal fisheries. This industry currently generates about 100,000 direct jobs, more than 90 percent of which are in small-scale fishing. Overall, about 600,000 people work in fishing and related industries. It is an important generator of jobs for the rural population and for women, who often are involved in cooperatives.

Canoes, wharves, and smokehouses dot the 250-mile (530-kilometer) coastline of Senegal. Saint-Louis, in particular, is known for its large fishing community. Its beaches are always covered with boats and racks for drying and smoking fish and have numerous food markets and places where boat builders ply their trade. Beaches are a ferrying point for the ocean-going cutters and large motorized canoes that can carry as many as 50 people.

More than half of the people living in Senegal's coastal villages earn their income from fisheries, and in some villages,

These fishermen in Kayar, Senegal unload their fresh catches of the day and rush them to market. Fish is a major part of their diet and about 600,000 people work in fishing and related industries.

more than 80 percent of the people depend directly on fishing. Part of the catch is sold fresh (for export and local consumption), and women do most of the work for this, processing and marketing the fish. A much larger part of the catch is processed by drying, salting, or smoking to preserve it for distribution to local and regional markets many hundreds of miles away.

Most of the fishing is done traditionally. Fishing practices have modernized little beyond the use of outboard motors and synthetic-fiber nets. Fishermen use many technologies in their trade, including homemade nets and traps. A typical Senegalese fishing boat is a 100-foot (30-meter) canoe of made of brightly painted wood. Many fishermen paint their vessels with the name of their favorite marabout. This ceremony is said to protect the fishermen, who often are at sea for four to five days during a fishing trip. During these trips, the fishermen cook on open fires in their boats; in some cases, these fires have gotten out of control and burned the boats. The work is dangerous. In places, death rates among fishermen are alarming, in part because they cross treacherous waters resulting from coastal and river mouth sand bars.

Senegal's government derives direct income from fishing. Substantial amounts are paid to the government through taxation, import and export levies, licenses, and fishery agreements. The most controversial are agreements with foreign nations. Under a recent fishing agreement with the European Union, Senegal received more than 32 billion CFA in direct financial compensation.

Overfishing remains a major threat. About 70 percent of the common species are in danger or already depleted. Tuna stocks, considered a standard for the sea's overall health, have almost disappeared. Decrease in fish off of West Africa is linked to European vessels legally fishing, as well as to Russian and Asian boats that slip in illegally. Since 2002, Senegal has banned vessels from the European Union from fishing in its waters after overfishing led to a crisis for the local industry.

Fishing communities are seeing their catches diminish sharply. Fishermen used to travel just a mile or two (two to three kilometers) off the coast of Dakar to catch fish. Now they must travel at least 7 to 12 miles (12 to 20 kilometers) out to sea in order to have a chance of catching fish. They also must stay at sea longer to fill their nets. Today, it takes fisherman 5 to 10 days to make a catch that used to take only one day. The quality of the catches also is changing, with commercially valuable species becoming increasingly scarce. Much of the blame is placed on foreign fishing fleets, but conservationists say that Senegalese fishermen must bear some responsibility. Many locals keep small fry rather than throwing them back or use dynamite instead of nets and hooks.

Forestry

Like other countries in the Sahelian region, Senegal is losing its forest cover at an alarming rate. Major causes are drought and harvesting wood for fuel. Increasing urbanization is accelerating forest degradation, because increased fuel wood consumption is linked to urban population growth. Charcoal production and bush fires also cause problems. Construction lumber is not locally produced but instead is imported.

In 1995, an estimated 39 percent of Senegal was forested. From 1990 to 2000, forest cover decreased at an estimated rate of 7 percent annually. Most remaining forestlands are dominated by woodland and savanna of varying types—wooded or a combination of trees, shrubs, and grasslands. There are some relics of dense rain forest and degraded gallery (river valley) forests.

Senegal is trying to protect its remaining forest resources and promote planned reforestation. Forest managers try to conserve forests and maintain an ecological balance. Their task is difficult, however, because they must also meet the peoples' needs for wood and nonwood forest products, including those obtained from wildlife. Senegal's forests are significant sources of economic benefit: People work forest plots, graze livestock, collect honey, and gather wild fruits and wood for various uses. Today, forests are a popular ecotourist destination. These activities are largely noninvasive and are considered part of normal forest management.

Innovative programs in which local peoples are recruited to manage forests near their towns and villages have been created. The people agree to certain restrictions in cutting and burning within forest boundaries in return for grazing rights and other uses of forestlands.

Industry

In former French West Africa, only the Côte d'Ivoire is more industrialized than Senegal. Industry contributes about a quarter of the country's GDP and employs about 12 percent of the work force. Light industries, most of which produce products for domestic consumption, dominate. The main industries involve processing of agricultural products and production of food and beverages. Mining and petroleum production, milling, manufacture of textiles, and commercial vehicle assembly are other activities, as are the production of farming materials (implements and fertilizers), paint, cement, printing, and boat building. The only heavy export industries are an oil refinery at Dakar-Mbao and the fertilizer and chemical industry that is based on imported sulfur and Senegalese phosphates.

Mining

Phosphates dominate the Senegalese mining industry, and the country is one of sub-Saharan Africa's major producers of this mineral. Most of the phosphate rock is processed domestically and converted to fertilizers and phosphoric acid. Even so, phosphate exports are a major earner, accounting for an estimated 16 percent of exports and approximately 2 percent of the nation's GDP. Most of the phosphates are exported to Canada, Australia, Mexico, and China. The phosphate deposits and production are scattered around the country.

Other mineral resources include iron ore, gold, oil, gas, and possibly diamonds. Large-scale, good quality iron ore deposits have been identified at Farangalia, Goto, and Faleme. The Faleme iron ore deposit, in southern Senegal, has reserves estimated at 391 million metric tons. None of the deposits are being mined at this time. In order to develop the Faleme deposit, port facilities will have to be built in Dakar and 460 miles (740 kilometers) of rail line will have to be upgraded or built.

Gold is produced in minor amounts. Many foreign companies have active exploration permits and are exploring for gold and diamonds in the southeastern part of the country, where ancient metamorphic rocks are exposed. Exploration so far has been disappointing. Both minerals have been discovered in small amounts but not in concentrations sufficient enough to consider mining in the area.

Senegal is not a major oil-producing nation. It does share management of an offshore oil field with Guinea-Bissau and has small onshore reserves. An active program of offshore exploration that may bring positive results is being pursued.

Tourism

Senegal has a growing tourist industry. After fishing, it is the country's second-largest provider of foreign currency. Currently, Senegal hosts about 400,000 tourists per year; this is expected to increase to 700,000 by 2006, when a new international airport will open outside of Dakar. Resort facilities have been developed in two main areas: in Casamance (Cap Skirring) in the south and in the area centered on Mbour, between Dakar and Joal.

Beaches in the Cap Skirring area are some of the finest in Africa. Originally a fishing village, Cap Skirring is located about 40 miles (70 kilometers) east of Ziguinchor in the Casamance. It is home to most of Senegal's tourist hotels and, except for the Gambia, hosts the highest concentration of foreign tourists in West Africa. About 30 years ago, French tourism organization Club Méditerranée (Club Med) established a resort in the far southwestern corner of Senegal. Since then, Cap Skirring has been marketed as a premier West African tourist resort, offering beach vacations to thousands of visitors from Western Europe and elsewhere. Cap Skirring receives charter flights from France and Italy, and the small airport plays another crucial role, enabling visitors to bypass the rest of Casamance. This ensures that Cap Skirring remains a privileged enclave, largely untouched by the 20-year civil war still being fought in the south. Elsewhere, cruise ships often dock at Dakar, and the city is served by the country's international airport.

Technology Sector

Information technology is a growing sector of Senegal's economy. The country achieved full Internet connectivity in 1996, creating a miniboom in information technology–based services.

7

Living in Senegal Today

S enegal is a truly exciting place to live and visit, full of contrast-ing lifestyles. Dakar and the larger towns are modern, whereas rural Senegal represents the traditional life. Senegalese people likewise are an intriguing mix of the modern and traditional, with a culture enriched by ethnic diversity. With a proud heritage, Senegal's people bring a rich legacy of food, fashion, music, dance, theater, art, and sport to the modern world.

SENEGALESE FOOD

Senegal is said to have the best cuisine in all of West Africa. The influence of French cooking traditions is unmistakable, especially in regard to the choice of seasonings—lemon juice, scallions, garlic, and marinades—for various dishes. Senegalese food also has a quality of its own, incorporating dishes from Europe and Asia and other parts of Africa.

Diet varies with wealth and other circumstances. Poorer Senegalese eat much simpler fare. In rural villages, families often are satisfied with a bowl of rice or millet accompanied by a few vegetables, a little fish, and a small piece of meat shared among the many members of the family.

Most Senegalese dishes include a starch base such as rice or couscous (made from grain, flour, salt, and water) accompanied by meat (usually beef, chicken, lamb, or fish) and vegetables (cabbage, carrot, cassava, and yam). Many local dishes are based on fish and rice. The most common dish today in the cities, especially at lunchtime, is *thieboudienne*, cooked rice accompanied by fish and vegetables stewed in a tomato sauce. It is considered a national dish, as are *poulet yassa* (chicken marinated in onion and lemon juice over rice), and *mafe* (groundnut sauce over steamed rice). The firm, fine-fleshed thiof, of the grouper family, is the preferred fish for thieboudienne. Since the devaluation of the CFA, few Senegalese can regularly afford thiof; most of it is exported. *Kaldou* is a regional fish dish from the Casamance. It is fish prepared with palm oil, vegetables, and rice accompanied by a lemon sauce.

Fresh seafood is available throughout the year in coastal towns and villages. The catch includes monkfish, sole, sea bream, red carp, Atlantic bumper, ray, grey mullet, shark, barracuda, and tuna, as well as prawns and lobsters, depending on season.

Meats are beef, lamb, and chicken. There is little pork in Senegal, because most Senegalese are Muslims. Expense keeps most Senegalese from eating beef and lamb. As in many other developing countries, chicken has taken the place of more costly red meat. There are many popular meat dishes, however. A favorite meat dish is *thiep bou yapp*, which is meat with rice in a sauce made with palm oil and tomatoes. The marketplaces are a great place to find meat dishes; there, you can buy brochettes wrapped in spicy mixtures and beef and lamb strips grilled over a wood fire. Pork is found in only in the south of country among the non-Muslim Diola. A popular local dish is oven-cooked suckling pig.

Rice is a staple. Senegalese prefer broken rice, which is cheaper than whole rice and is more appreciated for its taste. Wheat also has become part of Senegalese diet. It is usually in the form of bread and the "Moroccan," or wheat-based, couscous. Fresh bread, often baked over wood fires, is available in every village and in all neighborhoods. Couscous is made from a variety of cereal grains and is a basic food. In traditional villages, it is eaten almost every day, accompanied by peanut or tomato sauce with either fish or meat. In northern and central Senegal, couscous made from millet is a traditional dish. Its taste varies from sour and fermented in the center of the country to sweet in the northern regions. Mashed millet with sour milk and groundnut sauce also is commonly eaten. Corn-based dishes (couscous, porridge, and grits) are found in the south. Fonio, or hungry rice, the oldest of the African cereals, is appreciated today in Casamance and parts of east-central Senegal.

Senegalese use large quantities of oil in their cooking. Senegal produces peanut oil, but most of it is exported. Most cooking oil is the imported and less costly vegetable oil. Palm oil is used to some extent in the Casamance. This oil is extricated from the fruit of a variety of palm tree and has a special taste. Some people who are not used to palm oil find it hard to digest.

Senegalese enjoy vegetables and fruit with their meals. Vegetables are used primarily for flavor and are consumed in small quantities. Common vegetables are carrots, cabbage, turnips, manioc, okra, and bitter eggplant. Popular spices and flavorings include maggi, bissap leaves, netetou seeds, tamarind fruits, as well as dried and smoked fish. Meals often end with fruit. Senegal is not a large producer of fruit, although mangoes, grapefruit, papaya, oranges, lemons, melons, and guavas are grown locally. Bananas and pineapples are imported.

Eating at Home

Large meals are the general rule in Senegal. They are prepared to feed a large family and any drop-in guests. Food

This extended family is enjoying lunch out of a communal bowl. People eat with their right hands; Muslims consider the left hand unclean.

is served out of a large communal bowl, with the rice or couscous on the bottom and the toppings above. It is very important for the food to be appealing to sight and smell as well as taste. People sit on floor mats to eat and remove their shoes before sitting.

Silverware is not used; instead, people eat with their right hand. (Muslims consider the left hand impure.) A bowl of water is provided before and after the meal for the washing of hands. You can eat only what is in front of you, so it helps to imagine that you're slicing the meal like a pie. A good start is to roll up a little rice in the palm of your hand and put it into your mouth. Throughout the course of the meal, the server (usually the cook) breaks off choice pieces of fish and vegetables from the center and tosses them in front of the people eating because stretching to get food is thought to be rude. Beverages are served only after the main course. Alcohol is forbidden in the Islamic faith.

Meal Times

Most Senegalese eat three meals a day. A typical breakfast might include herbal tea, butter on French bread, and milk. Midday meals often consist of rice with fish, sorghum porridge, or grits with milk. Dinner, or the evening meal, might include stewed meat in a sauce over sorghum, couscous, or fried fish. In the rural areas, breakfast consists of leftovers from the previous night's dinner or porridge or grits with milk. Villagers tend to eat more locally grown cereals, whereas city dwellers are accustomed to imported rice.

Most people drink water after a meal. For visitors, there are always drinks made out of fruits such as mango, ginger, guava, the fruit of a rubber tree, the fruit of the baobab tree, or industrially made soft drinks. The most common local soft drink is extracted from bissap. After meals, guests may share kola nuts.

Tea, often prepared on a small charcoal burner, follows most meals, but it is not consumed exclusively with meals. During the day, a family and frequent guests may spend an hour or two drinking slowly from three small glasses of a sweet hot concoction of Chinese green tea and peppermint leaves. If you accept the first cup of tea, you must go to the third one, which is the sweetest. Light snacks consisting of salted roasted peanuts, fresh bread, or dried meat may be consumed as well.

Eating Out

There are many traditional and nontraditional options for eating out in Senegal. Local restaurants are called *tangana*, which means "hard and spicy." Tangana are informal places to enjoy a freshly roasted piece of meat. Traditionally, a chef is situated in a central location with a ready fire and grills lamb that is served in a bowl. There are also fish and rice dishes.

Seating in the tangana is communal. People sit on benches at the table and share the food with others in the restaurant.

There are more formal and westernized restaurants in Senegal, where a combination of Senegalese and French cuisine is served. These restaurants often serve European dishes prepared in a Senegalese way. Seating arrangements are westernized, with separate tables and silverware. The waiter takes the order and brings individual dishes to each person.

Because the Senegalese prize their own cuisine to such a high degree, there is little market for international restaurants. They are, however, fond of Lebanese fast foods such as *fatayers* (meat-filled fritters) and *chawarmas* (sandwiches with meat, French fries, tomatoes, onions and a sesame-based sauce). International restaurants exist mainly for travelers. One can find Thai, Indian, and Turkish restaurants, as well as French and Middle Eastern, in major cities and resort areas.

DRESS AND FASHION

Senegalese dress represents a wide array of fashion tastes and traditions and both traditional and Western styles. Dress varies depending on the occasion. Many people wear traditional clothing. Men may wear *boubous* or caftans to the mosque on Fridays (the Islamic holy day), to funerals, to work, and on Muslim holidays. The grand boubou is an ankle-length robe, which often has embroidery on the collar and sleeves. Men wear matching pants underneath their boubous, and women wear matching ankle-length skirts. Men sometimes wear shorter boubous that extend only to the waist.

Many women wear three-piece outfits made of colorful fabrics. On the bottom, they usually wear long, narrow skirts. On the top, they wear matching blouses, which come in many different styles. Some have low backs and ruffled sleeves; others are long-sleeved and off the shoulder. On their heads, women wear elaborately tied matching scarves. Sandals or leather loafers complete the outfit. The basic fabrics are local cottons.

Printed fabric is worn for everyday life, and dyed or hand-woven fabrics are reserved for special occasions.

In keeping with their status as mothers, educators, and authority figures for children, married woman generally wear more traditional outfits, although many include skirts, blouses, suits, and high heels in their wardrobes.

It is common to see Senegalese—especially younger people—wearing jeans, T-shirts, jean skirts, tank tops, suits and ties, shorts, and baseball caps. People buy this Western-style clothing in stores but have tailors and dressmakers make boubous and other forms of traditional clothing. Dakar's Sandaga Market has dozens of stalls that sell patterned and plain fabrics. Tailors at the market sew the fabrics into boubous and other clothing.

Hairstyles vary with age and ethnic identity. Women's hairstyles are often elaborate. Even when only a few months old, girls may have braids ornamented with beads and other small objects. Jewelry, made in gold, silver, iron, and copper, is another important element of dress.

Senegalese men and women are at the forefront of fashion in sub-Saharan Africa. Senegal is home to several cutting-edge designers, including well-known women designers such as Sadiya, Cole Ardo Sow, and Oumou Sy. Senegalese tailors, hair-dressers, and jewelers are among the most talented people exported to Africa, Europe, and the Americas.

MUSIC

Senegalese musicians play live music ranging from mbalax, the national pop style of Senegal, to jazz. There are many other traditions and style of music, such as Yela and different types of Western music including jazz, blues, salsa, rock 'n roll, and rap and hip-hop. Rap and hip-hop groups use music as a vehicle for voicing their concerns about Senegalese social conditions. They often take influences, including fashion, jewelry, manner-isms, and language, from American rappers.

The base of all music in Senegal is traditional. Contemporary Senegalese rhythms, such as the Yela, come from the old empires and predate French colonization. These rhythms still resound in music such as that of Baaba Maal. Senegalese kings used Yela to call the people of their empires together to hear important events. It is the music of women, because it mimics the sound they made when pounding grain Jimmy Cliff heard Yela when he visited Dakar; it is said to be the primary influence behind the development of reggae in the Caribbean.

Ibra Kassé, who founded the Star Band de Kakar in the early 1960s, is considered the father of modern Senegalese music. Foremost among today's stars is Youssou N'Dour, who combines traditional mbalax music and Western pop, rock, and soul and has an international following. Touré Kunda is another world-famous exponent of mbalax, and Baaba Maal, a Peul from northern Senegal, sings in his native tongue and displays a more traditionally "African" sound.

Formerly, music was limited to the griot. The Conservatoire de Musique, de Danse et d'Art Dramatique in Senegal first admitted only those of griot families but had to change its admittance policy. Traditionally, only a griot had the right to touch a musical instrument or perform in public. Society looked down on anyone else who dared to play or perform. Barriers are breaking down little by little as musicians and actors from other social classes are accepted and admired. Senegalese entertainers Baaba Maal, Omar Pene, and Ismael Lo are nongriot artists.

Griots continue to dominate popular music in Senegal. Today, more than two-thirds of popular instrumentalists and more than 90 percent of the popular singers are griots. A few contemporary well-known griot musicians include Youssou N'Dour, Fatou Guéwel, Thione Seck, and Bada Seck. Youssou N'Dour is a modern-day griot whose collaborations with musicians such as Peter Gabriel, Neneh Cherry, Branford

Senegalese percussionist Doudou Ndiaye Rose and his group of musicians play on the historic Gorée Island in April 2004.

Marsalis, Sting, and Paul Simon have made him one of Africa's most important and world-renowned performers. Singer Fatou Guéwel blends traditional and modern elements. Her praise songs have made her a favorite of rich patrons. Thione Seck began his career performing traditional music with the Ensemble Lyrique National at Sorano. Now he leads two groups: one modern (*Raam Daan*) and one traditional. Bada Seck is the lead drumming griot of Senegalese wrestler Mohammed Ndao (nicknamed "Tyson").

Griots use their traditional talents to provide entertainment for the growing tourist industry and also work on radio or television. It is certain that, without griots, there would be no musical heritage in Senegal. This class was responsible not only for making the music and songs but also for making the instruments themselves, including the *kora*, the violin-like *riti*, the *hoddu*, and the 7-stringed African guitar.

DANCE

In modern Senegal, many occasions—a wrestling victory, the harvest, a baptism—are pretexts for a dance party. Dance and wrestling parties offer a magnificent opportunity for singles, lovers, and friends to meet. Usually, every suburb, village, or age group has some kind of organizing committee to plan the date, the band, and the invited patrons. The date is important because some days are not allowed; there are no dances during the farming season, for example. The band consists of at least three and usually five to seven professional drummers. Sometimes another instrument, African or European, is added. The venue is a sandy area in the middle of the village or at some crossroads in the town. The youngest sit on the sand in the inner circle. Behind them, the women sit on chairs and benches or stand. Men stand on the outer circle. Boys and females do the clapping, sometimes using wood or metal clappers. The band plays at a corner of the inner circle, facing the most distinguished patrons, who are dressed in their best clothes. These patrons give money to the band members and the best dancers.

The dancers move in and out of the dance circle with no break in the dancing. Normally, only women, girls, and young boys dance, but men dance also in the Wolof country. Elsewhere, in the south and the east, religious and age-related ceremonies, such as initiations, offer men and boys in their teens the opportunity to dance. In cities like Dakar, Thiès, and Saint-Louis, there is a bustling nightlife with numerous discothèques, nightclubs, bars, and performing centers. There are also many popular dances, such as *gësëm*, mayonnaise, *cravache d'or*, or *jalgati*, created either by Senegalese artists or ordinary people.

SPORTS AND RECREATION

Football (soccer) is the most popular sport in Senegal. Young boys play it on the beach and in city streets. Its popularity was fueled even more when Senegal proceeded to the quarterfinals of the 2002 World Cup competition. The soccer team, the Gainde (Lions), had the best showing of any African country in the tournament's history. Basketball is gaining popularity, although more as a recreational sport. Racing enthusiasts in Senegal and abroad look forward each year to the Paris-Dakar cross-country rally. This is one of the longest and toughest off-road rallies in the world.

Senegalese also enjoy two sports considered indigenous: canoe racing and wrestling. Canoe racing draws large, excited crowds. Specially designed dugout canoes are painted in bright colors and named after a patron, usually a saint, local hero, or celebrity. In return, the patron provides spiritual protection or money. The races are organized by the size of the rowing team, between 6 and 36 men. Teams represent villages or suburbs. Rowdy fishermen often fight at the end of the event.

Wrestling, a traditional sport very much liked by the Senegalese, transcends all ethnic groups. Matches are accompanied by displays of amulets, drumming, dancing, and good humor. It is popular in rural as well as urban communities, and usually, villages or suburbs invite each other for tournaments. Matches often are held in sandy, open-air arenas.

Hours before the actual event, the beat of the drum and the voices of the singers alert everyone. In the late afternoon, a crowd gathers, forming a circle around a sandy arena. Children sit in the inner circle while adults stand at the outer edge, dressed in their finest clothes. Betting among the observers is common. Several bouts take place before the last one pits two champions against each other. The champions always represent two different teams fighting for prizes, supremacy, and prestige.

The rules are simple: The winner must make his opponent's knees, shoulder, or back touch the sand. In professional wrestling, blows and slaps are allowed and the prize is big money. In Dakar and other cities, modern stadiums are used to accommodate huge crowds. After a fight, the victorious side celebrates all night long and the victor's name is celebrated by songs.

Senegalese people enjoy swimming at the beach. Some of the Senegalese children play tag, hopscotch, and basketball and jump rope. Storytelling, Islamic festivities, and checkers are also common activities.

THEATER AND FILM

Theater is popular in Senegal. Today, many griots participate in the theater. Through its quality and its diversity, Senegalese moviemaking has led the African film industry. Senegalese filmmakers have made more than 250 films, about 30 of them full length. Filmmakers Ousmane Sembene and Djibril Diop Mambety have earned international respect for their work. Even they have faced obstacles in the distribution of their films, however.

Ousmane Sembene is known as Africa's greatest film-maker. Now more than 80 years old, he claims the title "Father of African Filmmaking." He is the first film director from an African country to achieve international recognition. Sembene established himself as one of Africa's leading novelists before turning to cinema as a way of reaching a wider audience. His films address a broad range of subjects, including the history of Senegal and the reality of Senegalese life. They vary in setting and period—from urban to rural and from the nineteenth century to World War II to the present day. His work often centers on identity problems encountered by Africans caught between Africa and Europe, tradition and modernization. *Ceddo* (1977), Sembene's masterpiece, is about a debate between the Muslims and the Christians of a village over how a bandit's kidnapping of the chief's daughter should be handled.

Djibril Diop Mambety also has had a major impact on Senegalese moviemaking. He was a director, actor, composer, poet, and speaker, loved and admired by critics and audiences all over the world. His work was highly experimental for its time.

MODERN LITERATURE

Senegalese people have been important contributors to literature. Léopold Sédar Senghor not only was president of the Republic of Senegal from 1960 to 1981; he also is also Africa's most famous poet. A cofounder of the Negritude cultural movement, he is recognized as one of the most significant figures in African literature. His poetry abounds with imagery and contrasts the lushness and wonder of Africa's past with the alienation and loss associated with colonization and assimilation into European culture.

In addition to Leopold Sedar Senghor, several authors have made major contributions to twentieth-century Senegalese literature. They include Birago Diop, Ousmane Socé, Alioune Diop (who founded the review *Présence Africaine*), Sheik Anta Diop, Boubacar Boris Diop, Mariama Bâ, and Ousmane Sembene.

ARTS AND CRAFTS

Each region of Senegal has its own traditional crafts, and the country is famous for its talented artisans, who can be found in the major markets, creating and selling their wares. Antique beads and large amber necklaces, traditionally worn by the Peul women, can be found in the markets and urban antique shops.

The blacksmiths constitute the artisan group that traditionally made tools, jewelry, and other items from iron, gold, and other metals. Today, this group makes exquisitely crafted gold, silver, and bronze jewelry. Baskets, pottery, and handwoven fabrics with intricate patterns are recognized crafts. Senegal markets and craft stores offer a colorful array of locally printed cotton fabrics used for traditional and modern clothes.

These carpets and paintings reflect life in Senegal and are on display at a local crafts fair in Dakar. Each region of the country has its own traditional crafts and its own skilled artisans.

Glass painting is another Senegalese specialty. The technique of reverse painting on glass came to Senegal from Asia in the nineteenth century. Painters depict people's daily life with humor and talent and in vivid colors and a personalized style. Sand painting is another art form. Black, ocher, red, white, and gray sands from every region of Senegal are used to create original paintings. Of purely Islamic inspiration in the beginning, sand paintings gradually incorporated scenes of daily life and portraits of Senegalese heroes. Woodcarving also can be found in many urban markets and shops.

FESTIVALS AND PUBLIC HOLIDAYS

Senegalese celebrate a number of holidays, Muslim, Christian, and civic. Muslim holidays are observed throughout the Islamic world. The Islamic (or Hejira) calendar is 11 days shorter than the Western (Gregorian) calendar. Therefore, public holidays and festivals fall 11 days earlier each year, on different dates and, for some events, during different phases of the moon.

Feast of Tabaski is the name given to the festival of Aïd-el-Kébir in West Africa, and it is the biggest celebration of the year in Senegal. Tabaski honors the Prophet Abraham's proof of his obedience to God (Allah). Allah asked him to sacrifice his son, but just before Abraham began the sacrifice, Allah told him to offer a ram instead. To remember Abraham's offering, each family sacrifices a sheep on Tabaski morning. The remainder of the day is spent in prayer and celebration. Everyone wears new clothes, and parents give their children presents and money. People feast on the roast sheep and share the meat with others. They visit family and friends and give thanks to Allah.

The entire country becomes absorbed with preparations for Tabaski. A sheep must be purchased for sacrifice and new clothes bought for the family. Traveling merchants set up stands to sell knives, barbeques, and dishware. Lots of people are in the street, and money circulates fast and furiously. Many families go into debt for Tabaski. A sheep, after all, costs (U.S.) $190 and sometimes much more, as prices rise with demand.

Korité is a holiday that marks the end of Ramadan. Ramadan is another important Islamic celebration. During the lunar month of Ramadan, Muslims fast during the day and feast at night. Many restaurants in the country are closed during the day, and some have restrictions on smoking and drinking. In hot weather, fasting is very difficult, because people also cannot drink water. During the day, many Senegalese chew on sticks called *socc* to help control their hunger. Korité, the end of the fast, is an occasion for much celebration.

Independence Day, April 4, is the most important civic holiday in Senegal. It is commemorated with parades and canoe races. Christian holidays, such as Easter and Christmas, are celebrated by Senegal's small Christian population. Other festivals and events in Senegal include carnivals, the Paris-Dakar rally, and various art, film, and music festivals. In Dakar, Carnival is celebrated the Monday before Ash Wednesday; in Saint-Louis, it always takes place on December 24, the day before Christmas.

The Paris-Dakar Rally is a 6,200-mile (10,000-kilometer) motor race that begins in Paris and ends in Dakar. It is held each year around the second week of January. Annual arts and entertainment events, most with set dates, include the Arts du Sous-verre, a show of traditional and contemporary glass painting; Dak'Art, a show featuring painting, sculpture, and interior design from different parts of Africa; Le Printemps des Cordes, African festival of traditional string instruments; Recidak, an African film festival; and the Saint-Louis Jazz Festival.

DAILY LIVING

To visitors from developed countries who are used to running water, ever-present electricity, paved roads, durable cars, and working traffic lights, Senegal is a shock. Many of these conveniences are poor or lacking. Roads are dark at night, there are few functioning streetlights, and there is constant competition among vehicles, humans, and animals on the roadways.

Housing and Settlement

Housing in Senegal differs depending on whether you are in the city or in a small town. In Dakar, there are many apartment buildings built out of concrete blocks. Most of the buildings are between one and four stories tall, with only a few taller. Houses are likely to be one story and built around an open dirt courtyard. In the towns and villages near Dakar, most of the houses are concrete, but some are thatch. In rural areas, mud and thatch housing is dominant.

Inside, many of the houses have open courtyards where chickens, donkeys, goats, sheep, and even cows are kept. The residents string up clotheslines for laundry in their courtyards. Most people sleep on mattresses on the floor. In some areas, mosquito nets are draped over the mattresses to protect people. Only a few houses in smaller villages have running water.

In the rural setting, Wolof often live in a compound enclosed by a fence. Houses in these villages are made from mud and thatched with grass or palm leaves. A few of the more affluent Wolof families in the villages may have houses made of concrete blocks. The inhabitants of the compound are an extended family that includes a man, his wives and children, his brothers and their families, aged relatives, and unmarried sisters. In the urban setting, housing ranges from shantytowns to concrete structures, the latter perhaps built by an employer. The urban household may consist of a nuclear family with extended family members from the village who are seeking jobs or schooling opportunities. Some urban Wolof families own a "family home," which is a place where displaced nephews or divorced sisters may live. In this case, it is the responsibility of the wealthy members of the family to provide for the needs of those living in the family house.

Getting From Place to Place

Transportation takes many forms. Only about 10 of every 1,000 Senegalese owns a car (compared with 480 of every 1,000 in the United States). Most vehicles in the country are taxis. Minibuses, vans, and trucks account for much of the remaining traffic. Many people take taxis or share minivans to get from place to place. Some ride bikes, and others travel by donkey cart. Most people simply walk.

Relatively few Senegalese own cars and many make their way around in painted buses such as this one.

Buying Food

Most Senegalese buy their fruits and vegetables at local markets or from street vendors in cities. Some vendors display their goods on sheets spread out on the ground, and others use wooden carts. In Dakar, the modernistic Kermel Market is one of the city's largest produce markets. Western-style supermarkets like Score sell imported foods, which are extremely expensive. Most Senegalese people do their shopping at smaller markets, where the food is much cheaper.

CHAPTER 8

Senegal Looks into the Future

Despite its many challenges, Senegal looks to the future with some hope and optimism. Although ranked as one of the world's poorest countries, Senegal's economy is beginning to grow. Recent gains in the GDP are a sign that government economic policy is finally taking effect.

Senegal has shown the world that peaceful change in leadership is possible. President Senghor stepped down after 20 years in leadership and turned over the reins to Abdou Diouf; more recently, Diouf was defeated for reelection by President Wade from the opposition party, and the transition occurred peacefully.

With limited resources, Senegal must provide for its people and protect and sustain its fragile resource base. The country must raise living standards in rural areas. Most villages lack running water and electricity. In addition, agricultural productivity has been steadily declining: Total national cereal production is down

Despite their smiles, the future of Senegal's young people is in jeopardy because of their extreme poverty, high unemployment, and poor levels of education.

from more than 1.2 million tons of millet, sorghum, rice, and maize in the 1999–2000 agricultural season to just 835,000 tons in 2002–2003.

In many areas, the soil has eroded or become acidic. A succession of droughts hit hard in the late 1970s and early 1980s, bringing more environmental degradation and rural impoverishment. More recently, a strange mixture of floods in some locations and spotty rainfall in others has pushed major parts of the Senegalese country toward near-famine conditions.

Improving living conditions depends on many things, including increased agricultural production. Currently, the government is emphasizing the need to modernize Senegal's underdeveloped, low-input agriculture. The goal is to transform Senegal's subsistence peasants into productive market-oriented farmers. To achieve this goal, the government must invest more in rural infrastructure and public programs to safeguard farmers from markets fluctuation, droughts, and floods.

Health and education are major concerns. The government has a goal of universal basic education and has established specific targets for achieving increased enrollments. A number of joint programs between Senegal and international aid organizations are planned or in place to tackle health-related issues.

The future of Senegal's young people is in jeopardy. More than 20 percent of the population is 15 to 24 years of age. About 45 percent of the youth live in urban areas. Unemployment is high, and educational attainment is low. Job training programs need to be established to train unemployed and underemployed youth so that they can find jobs.

The richness of Senegal's cultural life is tempered only by the extreme poverty of many of its people. While traditional values are upheld, living standards must improve for the next generation of Senegalese. Contrasts between the affluence of Dakar and the poverty of the rest the country is striking. Dakar impresses some as big, crowded, and dirty, although exciting, and as a drain on country's resources. The city is, in fact, the major center of banking and commerce for West Africa, rivaled only by Abidjan (capital of Côte d'Ivoire) in its attractiveness to international business. Dakar and Senegal are benefiting from this position and should continue to do so well into the future.

Country Name	Senegal
Location	West Africa, bordering the North Atlantic Ocean, between Mauritania and Guinea-Bissau
Capital	Dakar
Area	75,749 total square miles (196,190 square kilometers); land area, 7,4132 square miles (192,000 square kilometers); water area, 1,618 square miles (4,190 square kilometers)
Land Features	Generally low, rolling plains rising to moderate relief in the southeast
Weather and Climate	Tropical, with hot, humid summer rainy season; winter dry season dominated by hot, dry harmattan winds
Major Water Features	Senegal River, Saloum River, Gambia River, and Casamance River; Lake Guiers
Natural Hazards	Seasonal floods, periodic droughts, sandstorms
Land Use	Arable land, 11.58%; permanent crops, .19%; other, 88.23% (1998 estimate)
Environmental Issues	Deforestation, overgrazing, soil erosion, desertification, overfishing, poaching
Population	10,580,307 (2003 estimate)
Population Growth Rate	2.56 percent (2003 estimate)
Total Fertility Rate	4.93 average number of children born to each woman during childbearing years (2003 estimate)
Life Expectancy at Birth	56 years (male 55, female 58) (2003 estimate)
Ethnic Groups	Wolof, 43%; Pular (Fulani, Toucouleur, and other Peul), 24%; Serer, 15%; Diola (Jola), 4%; Mandinke, 3%; Soninke, 1%; European and Lebanese, 1%; other, 9%
Religion	Muslim, 94%; Christian, 5% (mostly Roman Catholic); animist (indigenous beliefs), 1%
Languages	French (official); national languages: Wolof, Pular, Jola, Mandinka
Literacy	Total population: 40% (male, 50%; female, 31%) (2003 estimate)
Type of Government	Republic under multiparty democratic rule

Facts at a Glance

Executive Branch	Chief of state—president; head of government—prime minister and a Council of Ministers appointed by the prime minister in consultation with the president
Independence	April 4, 1960 (from France)
Administrative Divisions	11 regions, 34 departments
Currency	CFA franc
Labor Force by Occupation	Agriculture, 70% (No information available on breakdown for other 30%.)
Industries	Agricultural and fish processing, phosphate mining, fertilizer production, petroleum refining, construction materials
Primary Exports	Fish, groundnuts (peanuts), petroleum products, phosphates, cotton
Export Partners	India, 21%; France; 13%; Mali, 9%; Greece, 8%; Italy, 4%
Imports	Foods and beverages, capital goods, fuels
Import Partners	France, 27%; Nigeria, 9%; Thailand, 7%; United States, 5%; Germany, 5%; Italy, 5%; Spain, 4%
Transportation	Highways (total): 9,058 miles (14,576 kilometers); Paved, 2,654 miles (about 4,271 kilometers) including a little over 4 miles (7 kilometers) of expressways; railroads, 563 miles (906 kilometers) narrow gauge; airports, 20 (9 paved); ports and harbors, Dakar, Kaolack, Matam, Podor, Richard Toll, Saint-Louis, Ziguinchor

Primary source: 2003 CIA World Factbook, Senegal

Second to eleventh centuries	The Empire of Ghana flourishes.
800s	The Empire of Tekrur is founded.
1080	Islamization begins.
1200s	Jolof Empire rises in central Senegal.
1200s–1300s	The Empire of Mali is based in eastern Senegal.
1400s	The first Europeans (Portuguese) arrive and establish the first trading posts on the Cap-Vert Peninsula, at Gorée, Rufisque, and Joal.
1500s	The slave trade, organized by the Portuguese, begins.
1617	The Dutch settle at Gorée.
1626–1659	The French colonize the future site of Saint-Louis.
Late 1600s	Gorée is taken by the English, then by France.
1700s	The Moors introduce the Qadiriyya brotherhood to Senegal.
1758–1814	The English and the French fight over Saint-Louis and Gorée.
1814	Senegal is given to France by the Treaty of Paris.
1815	The slave trade is abolished.
1848	France emancipates slaves in all of its colonies.
1854–1865	Faidherbe becomes governor of the colony and launches the French advance inland along the Senegal River. Dakar is established. The kingdoms of Djolof and Kayor are overthrown.
1856	Toucouleur leader al-Haj Umar launches holy war (*jihad*) along the Senegal and upper Niger rivers to establish an Islamic state.
1882	The railway between Dakar and Saint-Louis is constructed.
1887	The Mourides brotherhood is founded.
Late 1800s	The Sy dynasty of Tijanes is founded in Tivouane.
1895	A central governing body for French West Africa, *Le Gouvernement général de l'Afrique Occidentale Française* (*A.O.F.*), is formed.
1904	Dakar becomes the capital of the A.O.F (French West Africa).
1956	Federation of West African states controlled by France is dissolved.

1960   On April 4, Senegal is recognized as an independent state within the Federation of Mali. On August 20, the Federation of Mali splits up. On September 5, Léopold Sédar Senghor is elected president of the Republic of Senegal.

1970   President Senghor appoints Abdou Diouf prime minister.

1976   In April the constitution was changed to allow three political parties, with three different philosophies to be established. Apart from the UPS (governmental party, which would later become the PS (Socialist Party), are founded Abdoulaye Wade's party, PDS (liberal-democrat party), and the PAI (African Party for Independence) (Marxist-Leninist party).

1978   On February 26, Léopold Sédar Senghor is reelected president of the Republic of Senegal; for the first time he had to face an opponent, Abdoulaye Wade, leader of the PDS, who polled 17% of the votes.

1980   Léopold Sédar Senghor leaves office in favor of Abdou Diouf. On January 1, 1981, Abdou Diouf takes office as president of the Republic of Senegal.

1982   The confederation of Senegambia is officially announced.

1983   On February 23, Abdou Diouf is officially elected president of the Republic; he polled 80% of the votes when he stood as a candidate opposite four other candidates, in a universal suffrage election. The National Assembly later passes a constitutional reform that abolishes the post of prime minister. In May, Léopold Sédar Senghor is elected member of the "*Académie Française*" (French Academy). In December in the Casamance, confrontations with the police caused the death of 24 persons; the persisting discords makes an armed intervention necessary.

1988   Abdou Diouf is reelected president of the Republic of Senegal polling more than 73% of the votes; his success is strengthened when his party wins the general elections by an absolute majority. The opposition takes issue over the results; riots and confrontation with the police cause a state of emergency to be declared.

2000   Abdou Diouf loses the presidential election. Abdoulaye Wade's election as president puts an end to 40 years of continuous power by the Socialist Party.

Barboza, Steven. *Door of No Return: The Legend of Gorée Island.* New York: Peguin/Cobblehill, 1994.

Beaton, Margaret. *Senegal (Enchantment of the World)* Connecticut: Children's Press, 1997.

Brownlie, Alison. *Senegal (Worldfocus).* Chicago: Heineman Library. 1996.

Clark, Andrew Francis, and Lucie Colvin Phillips. *Historical Dictionary of Senegal,* 2nd edition. Metuchen, NJ: Scarecrow Press, 1994.

Collins, Grace, Brenda Randolph, Janet G. Vaillant, and Alex Bostic. *A Man of Destiny: Léopold Sédar Senghor of Senegal.* Philadelphia Sights Production, 2004.

Harris, Colin. *A Taste of West Africa (Food Around the World).* Ontario, Canada: Thomson Learning, 1994.

Insight Guide Gambia & Senegal. Philip Sweeney, Editor. London: Insight Guides, 1999.

Koslow, Philip. *Ancient Ghana: The Land of Gold.* Langhorne, Pennsylvania: Chelsea House, 1995.

———. *Centuries of Greatness: The West African Kingdoms, 750–1900.* Langhorne, Pennsylvania: Chelsea House, 1995.

———. *Lords of the Savanna: The Bambara, Fulani, Mossi, Nupe & Wolofo (The Kingdoms of Africa).* Langhorne, Pennsylvania: Chelsea House, 1997.

———. *Songhay: The Empire Builders (The Kingdoms of Africa).* Langhorne, Pennsylvania: Chelsea House, 1995.

Quigley, Mary. *Ancient West African Kingdoms: Ghana, Mali, and Songhai.* Chicago: Heinemann Library, 2002.

Rinaldi, Ann. *Hang a Thousand Trees With Ribbons.* New York: Gulliver Books Paperbacks, 1996.

Sallah, Tijan, Gary V. Wyck (Ed.), and George Bond (Ed.). *Wolof (Senegal).* New York: Rosen Publishing Group, Inc. 1996.

Vaillant, Janet G., Brenda Randolph, and Grace Collins. *A Trumpet for His People: Léopold Sédar Senghor of Senegal.* Philadelphia: Sights Production, 1996.

Websites pertaining to Senegal.
http://www.halcyon.com/aseaberg/senegal.html

Senegal Online.
http://www.senegal-online.com/anglais/presentation/carte-geo.htm

Index

116

Index

118

Index

Index

Index

page:

9:	© Lucidity Information Design, LLC	56:	EPA/Nic Bothma/Associated Press, AP
13:	Courtesy the UN Cartographic Section, No. 4174 Rev. 3, January 2004	65:	Associated Press, AP
16:	New Millennium Images	69:	KRT/New Millennium Images
17:	New Millennium Images	72:	KRT/New Millennium Images
24:	New Millennium Images	78:	© Vince Streano/CORBIS
26:	New Millennium Images	82:	New Millennium Images
29:	New Millennium Images	85:	New Millennium Images
30:	New Millennium Images	93:	KRT/New Millennium Images
38:	New Millennium Images	98:	AFP/New Millennium Images
43:	Associated Press, AP	103:	New Millennium Images
49:	KRT/New Millennium Images	107:	New Millennium Images
54:	KRT/New Millennium Images	109:	KRT/New Millennium Images

Cover: New Millennium Images

JANET H. GRITZNER is a Professor of Geography at South Dakota State University at Brookings. She started her career as a cultural geographer, but now teaches courses in Geographic Information Systems (GIS). She has worked and traveled in a number of countries in Africa (e.g., Senegal, the Gambia, Botswana, Kenya) and the Caribbean (e.g., Jamaica, Antigua, Bahamas, Guadeloupe, Puerto Rico). She has long been fascinated by Africa and African culture life. She has spoken to many audiences about her work in Senegal, the Gambia, and Botswana. She hopes to return soon to Senegal to see friends, revisit old places, discover new ones, and again experience the sights, sounds, and smells of Africa.

CHARLES F. ("FRITZ") GRITZNER is Distinguished Professor of Geography at South Dakota University in Brookings. He is now in his fifth decade of college teaching and research. During his career, he has taught more than 60 different courses, spanning the fields of physical, cultural, and regional geography. In addition to his teaching, he enjoys writing, working with teachers, and sharing his love for geography with students. As consulting editor for the MODERN WORLD NATIONS series, he has a wonderful opportunity to combine each of these "hobbies." Fritz has served as both President and Executive Director of the National Council for Geographic Education and has received the Council's highest honor, the George J. Miller Award for Distinguished Service. In March 2004, he won the Distinguished Teaching award from the American Association of Geographers at their annual meeting held in Philadelphia.